CATALYST **1**
Writing from Reading

STEVE JONES
Community College of Philadelphia

SUZANNE KALBACH
Community College of Philadelphia

THOMSON

HEINLE

Australia • Canada • Mexico • Singapore • Spain • United Kingdom • United States

THOMSON

HEINLE

Catalyst: Writing from Reading 1
Steve Jones and Suzanne Kalbach

Publisher: *Sherrise Roehr*
Acquisitions Editor: *Tom Jefferies*
Director of Product Development: *Anita Raducanu*
Director of Product Marketing: *Amy Mabley*
Executive Marketing Manager: *Jim McDonough*
Associate Production Editor: *John Sarantakis*
Manufacturing Manager: *Marcia Locke*

Production Project Manager: *Cindy Johnson*
Photo Researcher: *Vickie Piercey*
Cover Designer: *Gina Petti*
Index: *Alexandra Nickerson*
Composition: *Publishing Services*
Printer: *Edwards Brothers*

Cover Image: © Getty Images

Printed in the United States of America.
1 2 3 4 5 6 7 8 9 10 – 11 10 09 08 07

For more information, contact Thomson Heinle, 25 Thomson Place, Boston, MA 02210 USA, or visit our Internet site at elt.thomson.com

ISBN-13: 978-0-6184-7478-3
ISBN-10: 0-6184-7478-1

ISE ISBN-13: 978-1-4240-1736-2
ISE ISBN-10: 1-4240-1736-X

Library of Congress Control Number: 2007923311

Photo Credits: Page 1: © Jose Luis Pelaez, Inc./CORBIS; page 2: © Tom & Dee Ann McCarthy/CORBIS; page 10: © Gareth Brown/CORBIS; page 17: © Heungman Kwan/CORBIS; page 18: © Richard T. Nowitz/CORBIS; page 25: © ROB & SAS/CORBIS; page 35: © Tribute to Diego Rivera 1998 City of Philadelphia Mural Arts Program/Jane Golden/Photo by Jack Ramsdale; page 40: © History of Chinatown 1994 City of Philadelphia Mural Arts Program/Arturo Ho/Photo by Jack Ramsdale; page 46: © Pornchai Kittiwongsakul/Getty Images; page 55: © Royalty-Free/CORBIS; page 56: © Chris Hondros/Getty Images; page 73: © Charles O'Rear/CORBIS; page 81: © Steve Vidler/SuperStock; page 83, top: © Gail Grieg/SuperStock; page 83, bottom: © William Gottlieb/ CORBIS; page 91: © Bernd Obermann/CORBIS; page 92: © Getty Images; page 111: © Kevin Fleming/CORBIS; page 131: © Royalty-Free/CORBIS; page 132: © Paul Barton/CORBIS; page 139: © Farrell Grehan/CORBIS.

Contents

Chapter 7: Paved with Gold? 111

Chapter 8: A Better World Through Sports? 131

Introduction

The Catalyst Series

Catalyst is a two-book writing series that fills a specific need for high-beginning to low-intermediate-level ESL composition students in college, university, or adult education programs. The authors developed these materials for use in their own community college programs because they were looking for academically-oriented material that was simultaneously sophisticated in its content, well-grounded in the best second-language pedagogy, and yet comparatively low in its language level. They used versions of these materials for some time in their own writing classes and, based on their positive experiences with them, they wanted to share them with the wider world of English language teaching.

The key aspects of the *Catalyst* series are:

Content All of the material in the books centers on the experiences of immigrants to the United States and makes connections from those experiences to academic disciplines. The chapter topics deal with goals and issues that the authors have become familiar with while teaching college ESL for many years. We know that students are more engaged in their writing when they are asked to write about topics that relate to their everyday lives (and dream lives!), and this engagement results in more learning. Although the focus is on urban, working-class students, students with other experiences and situations, including international students, will certainly benefit from these materials as well.

Vocabulary The reading sections in the series include the study of vocabulary. There is a special emphasis on groups of words that appear in the Academic Word List. This frequently-encountered academic vocabulary is studied and practiced with an eye toward future work in college courses in all fields.

Pedagogy The *Catalyst* series is somewhere between the traditional "rhetorical structures/grammar" and "strong process" approaches to teaching. Both approaches have good points, so it's wise to combine them pragmatically. The organization of texts is taught in a traditionally explicit manner, and students are expected to understand concepts such as topic, topic sentence, introduction, etc., and to impose those concepts on their writing. However, learning happens only when a context creates a need for a new concept or structure. Students benefit from specific guidance about the particulars of writing, but some of the deepest learning is done inductively. This considered mixture of approaches is reflected in the *Catalyst* series.

In these books, reading selections play a prominent role. Compelling readings at the appropriate level help students to become more engaged in their learning, and they also give students a chance to learn both "inductively" and consciously about the features they are studying. The readings serve as a "catalyst" to stimulate a reaction in writing from students. They will respond with their own thoughts about topics significant to them that they want to get on paper.

The integration of the grammatical and organizational points is very carefully managed within the process of writing. Students are first asked to *find and recognize* important features in examples of writing. Then they are asked to write on related topics, concentrating on meaning, rather than form. It is in the rewriting stage, when most of the issues of meaning have been dealt with, that students are asked to focus fully on the rhetorical and grammatical concepts they have studied and practiced.

Writing assignments in this series generally ask students to write more than one paragraph. We believe that beginning students can benefit from the study of basic ideas about the organization of written works, which are often left for more advanced materials.

In addition to the first readings in each chapter in the series, which are mostly short, personal narratives, the second readings are designed to introduce students to a more academic prose style. These academic readings may be at a level that is a step above that of the students, but they are designed to remain accessible. First, they are supported by graphic information, including photographs, charts, and maps. Second, the language is challenging but controlled.

Teachers are invited to ask their students to read the following student introduction to this volume in the *Catalyst* series. It outlines the key components of each chapter and gives a brief explanation of how the series links reading, composing, and the study of vocabulary and grammar.

To the Student

The title of our book, *Catalyst*, means "something that causes a big change to happen." We hope this book will help you make a big change for the better in your writing because you will want to write about the topics of each chapter. Readings in the book are based on the experiences of other students like you who came to the United States and now live in a new country with different customs and challenges.

Catalyst is a book for students who recently began to write in English. It is for students who plan to take college-level courses, so they need to learn about college writing while they learn basic English grammar, vocabulary, and composition. We hope that the readings in this book are interesting, and that the ideas about writing are clear and helpful to you.

Each chapter in this book has several sections. In each section, we will ask you to do similar kinds of activities in all the chapters. These are the sections in each chapter:

Exploring the Topic In this book, we always ask you to think and talk about the topic of the readings and writing assignments before you begin your work. This activity will help you remember what you already know or think about this topic. It will also give you some ideas about what to expect when you read about the topic.

Reading 1, Vocabulary, and Academic Words Each chapter has a reading that introduces the topic of the chapter. This reading is usually about a person's experiences. You should try to do this reading without using a dictionary. It is written to make it easy for you to understand the most important ideas.

In this section you also will have a chance to work with words that are used in the reading.

Discussion In this book, we always ask you to talk about what you read. We believe that this discussion is an important part of the writing process. When you talk, you practice new words and think of new ideas. This helps you to improve your writing. There are two ways to have discussions about the readings. One way is for the whole class to have a discussion together. Another way is for smaller groups of students to discuss the reading. You should try both of these forms of discussion, because both can be useful.

Composition Analysis In this section, you will study the organization of the things you read. "Organization" means a plan the writer has for putting ideas together. When you study how other people write, this can help with your own writing.

Writing 1 In the first writing assignments, you are asked to write a paper that is about the reading. You might write your opinion about something, or you might write about your own experiences.

Grammar The grammar topics will help you express your ideas more clearly in the writing assignments for each chapter. The examples of grammar points in this book come from sentences in the chapter's readings.

Rewriting 1 It is very important for students learning to write well to review their own writing and to learn to make it better. In this section, you are asked to look for changes you want to make in your paper.

Reading 2, Vocabulary, and Academic Words The second reading in each chapter is on the same topic as the first, but it is an academic reading. This means that it is similar to the kinds of reading you will do in college courses.

As with Reading 1, vocabulary sections follow this reading. They allow you to work with words that are common in college writing. After the work on vocabulary, you will work with sections on Discussion, Composition Analysis, Writing, Grammar, and Rewriting, just as you did in Part 1 of the chapter.

To the Teacher

Catalyst 1 is intended to be at or near the lowest level of academically-oriented ESL writing. This means that rhetorical patterns center on description, narration, comparison, and basic forms of argument, although combinations of these purposes (and others) naturally emerge from the situations we pose. In grammar, "beginning" to us means little subordination and little use of complex verb tenses. We have attempted to push the vocabulary in the readings to the lowest level that would allow discussion of the topics we were interested in. We have also painstakingly analyzed the readings for their use of Academic Word List vocabulary, and placed a special focus on members of those word families.

These are a few of the important features of *Catalyst 1*:

The book is "academic" in the sense that each chapter relates to a specific academic discipline. Writing assignments ask students to make use of the simple academic texts that they have read. At the same time, every effort is made to make the level within this academic context as low as possible: vocabulary and grammatical structures are carefully controlled.

The vocabulary in each reading has been analyzed for its frequency of appearance in general English, and also for its appearance in the Academic Word List. The great majority of the words in the readings are from the 1,000 most commonly used English word families. Words that are from families between the 1,000 and 2,000 most commonly used in English are reviewed in vocabulary activities. Words from the Academic Word List are practiced separately. Less commonly used words, when they appear, are glossed for students in footnotes.

We have also taken particular care with the level of the readings to balance interest, an academic focus, and a language level appropriate for beginning students. Following are some of the specific grammatical features of the readings:

- Verb tenses are generally limited to simple present, simple past, present progressive, and past progressive.

- Passive verb phrases are mostly limited to a small number of stock expressions; complexity of subordinate clauses is limited.

- Ellipsis of subjects and other elements of clauses are avoided in compound and complex sentences, e.g. "They came here and they lived here."

- There is limited use of anaphora, e.g. "at this time" or "this/these [noun]."

- A limited variety of quantity expressions for nouns are used: *many, some, more, most*.

Note that writing assignments in the book usually ask students to write more than one paragraph. We believe that beginning students can benefit from the study of basic ideas about the organization of written texts, which are often left for more advanced materials.

Acknowledgments

The authors express their admiration and thanks to Kathy Sands-Boehmer, who made it all possible for us, and to Annamarie Rice, Evangeline Bermas, and Joann Kozyrev, who have put so much energy and wisdom into this project. Thanks are also due to Susan Maguire, an early supporter of our work, and to Cindy Johnson, of Publishing Services, who contributed substantially to the creation of this series.

Others who have added to the good qualities of this book include our reviewers:

Nancy Boyer, *Golden West College*
Marianne Brems, *Mission College*
Quan Cao, *Palm Beach Community College*
Jennifer Castello, *Canada College*
David Dahnke, *North Harris Community College*
Aileen Gum, *San Diego City College*
HeeSang Kim, *Northern Virginia Community College, Annandale*
Keiko Kimura, *Triton College*
Jeanne Morel, *Highline Community College*
Gail Reynolds, *Santa Barbara City College*
Esther Robbins, *Prince George's Community College*
William Shoaf, *City College of San Francisco*
Lisa Stelle, *Northern Virginia Community College, Sterling*

We are also grateful to our students at Community College of Philadelphia, who have shaped this book over the years through their hard work and good humor, and who have entrusted us with their ordinary and extraordinary experiences as immigrants.

I am indebted to my colleague Grace Flisser, who has guided and supported me during the development of this book, and to Pat Jones, my ESL colleague, first teacher, friend, and mother.

Steve Jones
Philadelphia, Pennsylvania

I'd like to acknowledge my mother, Ann Shively Kalbach, who has taught me to love and respect language, and Dr. Virginia Allen, who transmitted to her students at Temple University her vast experience with and subtle insights about teaching English to speakers of other languages.

Suzanne Kalbach
Philadelphia, Pennsylvania

Catalyst 1: Scope and Sequence

Chapter Topics	Reading Topics	Composition Analysis and Writing Competencies	Writing Topics	Grammar Competencies
CHAPTER 1 **Personalities**	The personality of a student How people get their personalities	Topics of paragraphs	Description of your personality Composition about another person	Simple present tense
CHAPTER 2 **Marriage in different cultures**	Problems of dating and marriage Intercultural marriage	Topic sentences and main ideas Introduction paragraphs	Advice about a personal problem Report of several paragraphs	Modal verb *should* in affirmative and negative Subject, object, and possessive pronouns
CHAPTER 3 **Finding meaning in works of art**	A description of a mural The history of the mural movement	Organization of a description Conclusion paragraphs	Description of a scene Proposal for a project	Present progressive verb tense, in both affirmative and negative Modal verbs *can, may,* and *should*
CHAPTER 4 **City neighborhoods**	Rebuilding a neighborhood History of immigrants and neighborhoods	Narration Scanning and skimming	Business letter that gives reasons Description of a neighborhood	Simple past tense Quantifiers: *many, some, more, most*
CHAPTER 5 **The history of architecture**	A letter about a new home History of home building in the United States	Organization of a letter Chronological order	Personal letter about your home Composition about the architecture of a home	*there is* and *there are* Contrast expressions
CHAPTER 6 **Crime: its causes and solutions**	A narration showing several versions of the same event Causes of crime	Narration: topics and topic sentences Point of view	Narration that includes an opinion Composition about the causes of crime	Simple past tense with negative Cause and effect expressions
CHAPTER 7 **Immigrant life in the United States**	A letter about life in the United States The economic effects of immigration	Contrasting ideas Positive and negative information	Written response to an opinion about life in the United States Essay on economic life for immigrants in the United States	Comparative form of adjectives Contrast expressions used in transitions
CHAPTER 8 **The role of sports in bringing people together**	A story about sports and new immigrants Sports as a way to reduce conflicts	Narration: chronological order Main ideas and examples	Prediction about the future of a family Description of your experiences in a group	Future tense Review of verb tenses

1 Writing About Yourself

Exploring the Topic

ACTIVITY 1

Discussion In each chapter of this book, you will always talk with classmates about the topic before you start to read and write about it. Writing about yourself is the topic of the first reading and writing work in this chapter. The questions below will help you think about the ideas in this chapter. Discuss these questions with your class.

1. Who are you? Tell some important things about yourself.

2. Why do you want to study English writing and reading?

3. How do you feel right now? Are you nervous? happy? bored? excited?

Reading 1: Personal Experience Reading

In this chapter you will read a student's composition for his first writing assignment. A teacher asked her students to write about themselves and about some of the people who are important in their lives. She asked students to do their best writing in English. One student, named Sebastiano, started his paper by describing a little bit about his life. Later on, he wrote about his uncle, his own personality, and his father's personality.

Read Sebastiano's composition.

 ## My Life and Personality

1   My name is Sebastiano Colón. I came to this country about eight years ago. I live with my uncle on Springfield Avenue. I have a job in my uncle's store. His store is in our neighborhood, a few blocks from his house. I spend most of my time with my uncle and my cousins.

2   My uncle is a good man. He is quiet and serious. He works every day in his store. My uncle is very popular in our neighborhood. Everyone says that he is very helpful and generous. He is also a calm person. He takes care of me, and he shares everything with me. He says I am like his son.

3   I am very shy, and this has a big effect on my life. I am very quiet, and it is not easy for me to meet new people. I do not have many new friends in the United States. I have some friends at my job, but I don't see them outside of work. After work I just like to go home and read or listen to music. At home we

usually speak our language. I feel a little embarrassed because I have been in this country for a long time, but my English is not very good. Part of the reason is that I am shy.

4   People say that my personality is very different from my father's. He is a happy guy, and he always enjoys himself. He is very popular in our home town. Everyone knows him. He talks a lot, and he likes to meet new people. He does not worry about life. I am not like him. I am a serious person. I worry a lot about the future. I want to be more like my father!

Vocabulary

ACTIVITY 2   The words below are from the composition you just read. These vocabulary words are in the order they appear in the reading. For example, the first word in the list below is the first vocabulary word in the reading; the second word in the list appears second in the reading.

Work with a partner and write the meanings of the words on the lines that follow. If you do not know the meaning of a word or phrase, try to guess. Find the word in the story before you guess. The sentence where you see the word may help you to guess its meaning. If you cannot guess, try to find the correct meaning in the dictionary, or ask your teacher.

1. **serious** (adjective) _____

2. **shy** (adjective) _____

3. **embarrassed** (adjective) _____

4. **enjoys himself** (verb) _____

Discussion

ACTIVITY 3   **A.** Here is a list of words that can describe people. These words can describe people's feelings, and also their personalities. Your teacher can explain the meanings of the words. Which of these words describe you? What other words can describe you?

shy	funny	helpful	adventurous
happy	nice	calm	generous
serious	angry	mature	
relaxed	quiet	proud	
sad	nervous	outgoing	

B. Describe an important person in your life. Describe this person's personality. Are you different from this person, or are you the same?

Composition Analysis

Topic Good writers usually divide writing into parts or **paragraphs**. Each paragraph is about one idea. This idea is called a **topic**. Paragraphs usually have several sentences in them. The first sentence is **indented**; it starts a little to the right. **Indenting** is a sign that a new paragraph and a new topic are beginning.

Notice the form of this paragraph:

Indenting

2   My uncle is a good man. He is quiet and serious. He works every day in his store. My uncle is very popular in our neighborhood. Everyone says that he is very calm. He is also very helpful and generous. He takes care of me, and he shares everything with me. He says I am like his son.

The topic of this paragraph is "my uncle." This paragraph tells several things about Sebastiano's uncle and his personality. All of the sentences in this paragraph are about the same idea.

Notice that there are four paragraphs in Reading 1. (Each paragraph in the readings in this book has a number on the left side.) Each paragraph has its own topic.

| ACTIVITY 4 | Look at paragraphs 3 and 4 in Sebastiano's composition. Name the topic of each paragraph. The topic of paragraph 2 is given as an example. |

Paragraph 2:   *Sebastiano's uncle and his personality*

Paragraph 3:   _____

Paragraph 4:   _____

Writing 1

ACTIVITY 5 Practice writing sentences that describe different personalities. First, read the sentences that contain words to describe personalities. Then, write a sentence that gives an example of this kind of personality. The first one is done as an example.

1. She is very shy.

   She feels nervous when she meets new people.

2. He is outgoing.

   _____

3. They are very serious.

   _____

4. She is generous.

   _____

5. We are adventurous.

   _____

6. They are helpful.

   _____

7. He is mature.

   _____

8. I am quiet.

   _____

ACTIVITY 6 **Writing Assignment** Write a composition about your personality and the personality of a family member. Your composition can answer these questions: What kind of person are you? Is your personality the same as your family member in some ways? If so, how?

Before you write, think about the class discussion about personality. Review the vocabulary words on page 3. This vocabulary will help you get ideas for your composition. When you write, try to write one paragraph about each topic. In each paragraph, give examples of the word you use to describe yourself or your family member.

Use the chart below to help you think of ideas for your composition. Put a circle around the words that describe you and the other person you are writing about. Then write an example that explains each word. The first two lines are examples that show how to use the chart.

My Personality

Person	Adjective	Example
myself	(shy)	I don't like to talk in class.
my brother	(serious)	He does his work before he has fun.
	shy	
	serious	
	sad	
	happy	
	adventurous	
	helpful	
	funny	
	generous	
	mature	
	outgoing	

Now write your composition about yourself and another member of your family. You can write one paragraph about the ways your personality and your family member's are similar. Then write another paragraph about the differences between your two personalities. When you finish writing, put your paper aside for a while.

Grammar

Verb Tenses: Simple Present Tense

Look at these sentences from the reading:

1 I **live** with my uncle.
2 I **am** very shy.
3 He **is** a happy guy.
4 I **worry** a lot.

All of the sentences above contain verbs that tell about things that are usually, generally, or always true. They are not only happening now. These verbs are in the **simple present tense**. We often see them in sentences that also have frequency words. These are words that tell how often an action happens. Examples of frequency words are *always, usually, often, sometimes, seldom,* and *never*.

5 I seldom **worry**.
6 He always **enjoys** himself.

The simple present tense is also used to describe **feelings** or **thinking**:

7 I **think** my father is like that.
8 He **wants** to study computer science.
9 She **knows** he was tired.

The simple present tense is also used to describe how things **look** or **sound**:

10 I **look** like him.
11 He **seems** happy.
12 That **sounds** good.

Simple present tense verbs have a special form. Many times verbs in the simple present tense have no endings:

13 I **look** like him.
14 They **worry** a lot.

However, sometimes simple present tense verbs end with *-s*. If the **subject** of the sentence can be *he* or *she* or *it*, simple present tense verbs end with *-s*. Look at these examples:

15 He live**s** in New Jersey.
16 My teacher live**s** in Los Angeles. (This subject can be *she* or *he*.)
17 She seem**s** nice.

A. Write complete sentences to answer these questions. Check to make sure that you used the simple present tense correctly. Make sure that you write sentences, not short phrases. Use *she* or *he* as the subject. When you are finished, show your sentences to your teacher.

1. Where do you live?
2. Who lives with you?
3. What family member looks like you?
4. Who do you love?
5. What languages do you know?
6. What do you like to do for fun?
7. How do you usually feel on Saturday night?
8. How do you feel when you meet a new person?
9. What do you worry about?
10. What do you say when someone sneezes?

B. Next, ask a classmate the questions above. Write down your classmate's answers. Remember to put an *-s* on present tense verbs when the subject is *he* or *she*.

ACTIVITY 8

The paragraph below has some mistakes in simple present tense verb forms. Find the mistakes and make corrections. (You should find seven mistakes). Discuss your answers with your class.

My brother is very different from me. In general, he is a happy person. He talks to people all the time, and he always smile. He seem like he is very relaxed. He never worry. He like to go out with his friends. He works very hard, but he like to have a good time also.

My parents are more like me. They are very serious. Of course, they are nice people, but they prefers to stay home. They do not laugh or make jokes a lot. They are very generous and kind with their children, but they worry too much about us. They loves my brother, but they think he is not very mature.

Rewriting 1

Good writers usually write their papers more than one time. The first time you write, your paper is called a **first draft**. In your first draft, you should think mostly about getting your ideas on paper. When you rewrite your paper, you should make changes to correct it and make it clearer. Some of the changes might be corrections in grammar.

ACTIVITY 9

A. Read your paper from the writing assignment in Activity 6. Try to find the **topic** of each paragraph of your paper. Write the topic next to each paragraph on your paper. (There are examples of paragraph topics in Activity 4 in "Composition Analysis" above.)

B. Find all the verbs in your composition. Are some of the verbs in the simple present tense? Do the verbs have the right form? That is, should there be -s endings on some of the verbs because their subjects mean *he*, *she*, or *it*? Did you use frequency words like *usually* or *sometimes* correctly to show how often these actions happen?

C. You can use the checklist below to help you review the important things you want to include in your composition. Write "yes" or "no" as answers to the questions on the list.

CHECKLIST

Content
Did you describe your personality?
Did you describe your family member's personality?

Organization
Is your paper divided into paragraphs?
Do the paragraphs have clear topics?

Grammar
Did you use simple present tense verbs correctly?

After you review the checklist, rewrite your paper. Change your paper so that it is divided into paragraphs and each paragraph has a topic that you can name. When you finish rewriting, give your paper to your teacher.

PART 2

Reading 2: Academic Reading

This reading is similar to an academic reading in psychology. It explains ideas about personalities.

Where Does Personality Come From?

1   Psychologists study human behavior and human emotions. In other words, they study and describe personalities. When psychologists describe personalities, they describe ways that people are similar or different from each other in their actions or their emotions.

2   Personality "traits" describe the common behavior and feelings of a person. For example, some people like to take risks, and others avoid risks. These are personality traits. Other personality traits describe whether people often worry, or whether they have a strong religious feeling. When a person is shy, or when someone enjoys meeting new people, these are also examples of personality traits.

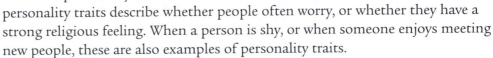

3   Psychologists ask questions about where personalities come from. They learn that personality comes partly from nature, or from genes. Genes are the chemical[1] instructions that come from the parents of a person, animal, or plant. Genes decide things like a person's hair color, eye color, height, and so on. When people have the same genes, they often have the same personality traits.

4   Scientists learn about the importance of genes in personality by studying twins. Even when identical twins are raised apart, they are very similar in their personalities. Often they are similar in how much they worry about things, how outgoing they are, or how much they take risks. Twins also usually have similar feelings. For example, they often have the same feelings about religion and music.

5   Part of personality also comes from what people learn from their early experiences. When people grow up in the same family, they often have similar personalities. Adopted children are often similar even though they do not have the same natural parents or the same genes. They often have similar feelings and behavior because they learned this behavior from an early age.

[1] *Chemical* means related to the basic elements that all things are made of.

6   Scientists believe that both biology (the traits people are born with) and environment (their experiences) help to form a personality. People can start their lives with traits that affect their personality. However, experiences in life will also change the development of personality.

Vocabulary

ACTIVITY 10   You probably already know the words below. They are listed in the same order as they appear in the reading. To check your understanding of these words, choose one of the words to complete each sentence below. After you are done, review your answers with your class.

behavior (noun)	**risks** (here, a noun)
apart (adverb)	**worry** (here, a verb)

1. He seems to _____ about small problems as well as big problems.

2. His strange _____ showed that he was tired and upset.

3. The two friends were always unhappy when they spent a long

    time _____.

4. He took a lot of _____ when he was young, but he never got hurt.

ACTIVITY 11   **Academic Words** Academic vocabulary means words that often appear in college textbooks in all subjects. They are not used as often in everyday English, especially not in speaking.

    Read the sample sentences below. They contain academic vocabulary in **boldface** (dark) letters that might be new to you. Then, in the sentences (a–d) that follow, choose the academic vocabulary word that fits best in each sentence. Review your answers with your class.

1. When something **affects** us, it causes a change in us.
2. The **environment** is everything around us.
3. If two people are **identical**, they are the same in every way.
4. **Psychologists** are scientists who study human thinking, feelings, and behavior.

a. The _____ were studying personality and beliefs.

b. The brothers were similar, but they were not _____.

c. The _____ in the city is usually noisy and crowded.

d. His early childhood _____ his personality as an adult.

Discussion

ACTIVITY 12 Review the personality "traits" that are mentioned in the reading, such as liking to take risks. Discuss the following questions.

1. What personality traits do you see in yourself or other people you know that probably come from genes?

2. What personality traits in yourself or those other people probably come from the environment?

Composition Analysis

Topic As you saw in Part 1, writers divide compositions into paragraphs, and each paragraph has a topic. Reading 2 has six paragraphs. The paragraphs are about the topics of personality, genes, experiences, etc.

When writers divide their compositions into paragraphs, it helps make their writing clearer. Each time a new paragraph begins, the reader knows that the writer has changed the topic. You should use your understanding of paragraphs to help you understand what you read, and to help make your own writing clearer.

ACTIVITY 13 Write answers to these questions about the reading.

1. In paragraph 1, the reading gives information about "personality." What information do we get about personality?

   _____

   _____

   _____

2. In paragraph 2, there are examples of personality traits. What are examples of these traits?

   _____

   _____

   _____

3. Paragraph 3 is about one thing that affects personality. What is the topic of this paragraph?

_____

_____

_____

4. Paragraph 5 is about a second thing that affects personality. What is the topic of this paragraph?

_____

_____

Writing 2

ACTIVITY 14 Practice writing sentences that describe people's lives and their personalities. Work with a classmate. Interview your classmate and ask him or her the questions below. Write sentences that are answers to the questions. An example is given for you.

1. Where do you live?

    *She lives on Northern Road.*_____

2. How many people do you have in your family?

    _____

    _____

3. What kind of work do you do?

    _____

    _____

4. What is one of your personality traits?

    _____

    _____

5. What is a personality trait of one of your family members?

_____

_____

<table>
<tr><td>ACTIVITY 15</td><td>

Writing Assignment In this writing assignment, you will write a description of a stranger. You will not write a true story; you will use your imagination to write about the personality and life of this stranger. You will spend a few minutes looking at the stranger and then think of a story about this person's life and personality.

</td></tr>
</table>

Find an interesting person in the grocery store, waiting in line somewhere, at your school cafeteria, or at your job. Look at the person and imagine what he or she is like. You don't have to speak to the person; just think of your own ideas about his or her life. Here are some of the questions you might answer in your paper: Where does the person live? What is his or her family like? What kind of work does the person do? What is his or her personality like? Is this stranger's personality similar to other people in the same family?

Your paper might begin like this:

Her name is Olga. She lives outside the city in a big house ...

When you have finished your paper, put it aside for a while.

Grammar

The Form of Simple Present Tense Verbs

Reading 2 explains some of the ways that people's personalities develop. It describes the work of psychologists, and it also explains how people usually behave. All of this information is in the **simple present tense**. Following are some examples of verb forms from Reading 2:

> Psychologists **study** human behavior and human emotions.
> Psychologists **describe** ways in which people are similar or different from each other.
> Some people **like** to take risks, and others avoid risks.
> Personality **comes** partly from genes.

When you read simple present tense verbs, you understand that these sentences are usually or generally true. Notice again that when the subject of a present tense verb means *he*, *she*, or *it*, the verb ends with *-s*.

ACTIVITY 16

In Reading 2, there are many verbs in the simple present tense. Find all the simple present tense verbs, and write them below. Find the subject of each verb. Write the subject next to the verb. Some examples are done for you.

Subject	Simple Present Tense Verb
psychologists	study
they	study

ACTIVITY 17

In the paragraph below, write the correct simple present tense of the verb in parentheses. Remember to add -s at the end of the verb if the subject means *she, he,* or *it*. The first one is done as an example.

Dr. Martin Young (1. be) _____*is*_____ a psychologist. He

(2. study) _____ human behavior at a university. Dr. Young

(3. describe) _____ the ways in which people (4. be) _____ similar

or different from each other in their actions or their emotions. Dr. Young is

interested in risk-taking. He (5. believe) _____ that some people naturally

(6. like) _____ to take risks. This is an example of a personality trait. Dr.

Young (7. think) _____ that risk-taking (8. come) _____ partly

from a person's genes. He (9. study) _____ groups of twins to find out if

people usually (10. learn) _____ to like risky behavior, or if they are

born with this trait.

Rewriting 2

ACTIVITY 18

A. Organization Read your composition about a stranger from Activity 15 again. Is your paper divided into paragraphs? Does each paragraph tell about a different part of the person's life? If not, change your paper. Rewrite it so that each paragraph answers a different question about the person. You may want to add some new details to your story when you rewrite.

B. Grammar Many of the verbs in your story should be in the simple present tense. Simple present tense verbs should be in the parts where you described general things about the person, or when you described the person's feelings. Underline each verb in your story. Did you use the correct ending for each verb? If you are not sure, you might get help from a grammar book, or you can ask your teacher.

C. When you are finished making changes to your paper, review the checklist below. If you answer "no" to any of the checklist questions, change your paper before you hand it in. When you are ready, hand in your paper to your teacher.

CHECKLIST

Content
Did you describe the person's life, including family, work, personality, etc?

Organization
Is your paper divided into paragraphs?
Do the paragraphs have clear topics?

Grammar
Did you use simple present tense verbs correctly?

Internet Activities

For additional activities related to this chapter, go to elt.thomson.com/catalyst.

 Family Pressures

Exploring the Topic

Discussion In this chapter, your teacher will ask you to talk with your classmates before you read and write about family pressures. Think about these questions:

1. Do you know anyone who married a person from a different country? Is the married couple happy together? How do their families feel about their marriage?

2. Do you think it is possible for people who marry a person from another culture to be happy in their marriages? Why or why not?

Reading 1: Personal Experience Reading

Here's a reading, based on a true story, about the problems of being in love with a person from another culture.

A Difficult Love

1   Binh is a 23-year-old Vietnamese woman who lives with her family in the United States. Her parents are quite old and don't speak much English. They like to follow the traditional Vietnamese ways even though they live in the United States. Binh studies at a college and works part-time.

2   A year ago Binh met a very nice young American man at her job. She started to meet him secretly when her parents thought she was at school. Little by little they fell in love. Now they have decided they want to get married.

3   Binh is afraid to tell her family about her American boyfriend because her parents do not allow dating. In traditional Vietnamese culture, parents usually choose a partner for their children, and then the children can accept their parents' choice or not. Binh is worried that her family will be angry because she is going out with this man without their permission.

4   Even worse, Binh is afraid that her family will never accept her marriage to a non-Vietnamese man. Her parents want their children to marry a Vietnamese person. Her parents do not have a good opinion of most young Americans, so she thinks they will not approve of her marriage to an American man.

5   Binh's feelings about her boyfriend are confused. She feels guilty because she is seeing this man secretly, and because she is lying to her family. However, she loves this young man very much. She feels terrible when she thinks about not seeing him anymore. She feels sure he loves her, too, and she thinks he will be a good husband and father. However, if she decides to marry him, her family may not want to see her anymore.

Vocabulary

ACTIVITY 2   You may already know the words below. To check your understanding of these words, choose one of the words to fit in each sentence. After you are done, review your answers with your class.

afraid (adjective)   **approve** (verb)   **worse** (adjective)
angry (adjective)   **worried** (adjective)   **guilty** (adjective)

When I was a little girl, I was very _____ of a big white dog in my neighborhood. The dog made an _____ noise every time I walked past his house. One day he came out of his yard into the street near me, and I screamed and ran home. My mother was very _____ about me because I could not stop screaming. She called the dog's owner and said, "I do not _____ of people letting their dogs run around outside!" Our neighbor told her, "I feel _____ because your daughter is upset, but don't worry. My dog won't hurt her—his bark is much _____ than his bite. He loves children!"

ACTIVITY 3   **Academic Words** Read the sample sentences (1–3) below. They contain academic vocabulary (in **boldface**, or dark letters) from Reading 1 that might be new to you. Each sentence shows the meaning of its academic word.

1. Each **culture** in the world has its own beliefs, habits, food, and clothes.

2. Work with another student in the class as your **partner** on this project.

3. It is not **traditional** in the United States for students to stand up when the teacher comes in.

Choose the academic word from the sample sentences that fits best in the sentences that follow (a–c). Review your answers with your class.

a. Turkey is a _____ food for Thanksgiving in the United States.

b. If you go into business with a _____, you should know that person very well.

c. Sometimes it is hard to understand another _____ because its people have different ways of thinking about life.

Discussion

ACTIVITY 4   Discuss these questions with a partner. Write notes about your answers on the lines below. When you are finished, tell the class what you think.

1. Should Binh tell her parents about her boyfriend? Why or why not?

_____

_____

_____

2. Should she stop seeing him if her parents don't like him? Why or why not?

_____

_____

_____

3. Should she look for a Vietnamese husband? Why or why not?

_____

_____

_____

Composition Analysis

Topic Sentence   Usually in English compositions we try to make each paragraph about one important idea or **main idea**. Usually there is one sentence in a paragraph that tells the main idea of that paragraph. This sentence is called the **topic sentence**. Often the topic sentence is the first or second sentence in the paragraph, but not always. All the other sentences in the paragraph should explain more about the topic. The other sentences give details or examples that help the reader understand the main idea.

Analyze paragraphs 3, 4, and 5. First, write the topic sentence of each paragraph that tells its main idea. Then write the details or examples that explain the important idea in that paragraph.

Paragraph 3

Topic sentence:

_____

_____

Details or examples:

_____

_____

_____

Paragraph 4

Topic sentence:

_____

_____

Details or examples:

_____

_____

_____

Paragraph 5

Topic sentence:

_____

_____

Details or examples:

_____

_____

_____

Writing 1

ACTIVITY 6 In the writing assignment for this chapter, you will write a composition about your advice on what Binh should do in her situation. To prepare for the assignment, write a paragraph that explains Binh's problem. Include answers to these questions in your paragraph:

1. Who is Binh's boyfriend?

   _____

   _____

2. Why does she not want to tell her parents about her boyfriend?

   _____

   _____

3. Why does Binh feel guilty about her boyfriend?

   _____

   _____

When you write the paragraph, you can use this topic sentence:

> *Binh is a Vietnamese woman who has a problem about her parents and her boyfriend...*

ACTIVITY 7 **Writing Assignment** Write a short, two-paragraph composition about one of the three questions under "Discussion" in Activity 4.

Use the paragraph from Activity 6 above as your first paragraph. In your second paragraph, give a direct answer to the "Discussion" questions. This is your topic sentence; it tells your most important idea. Then, in the rest of the second paragraph, explain your reasons for this answer. You can use your answers from Activity 4.

After you are finished writing and discussing your paper, put it aside. You will give it to your teacher after you make more changes.

Grammar

The Modal Verb *should*

The sentences below give some advice:

1 You **should** brush your teeth twice a day.
2 Young people **should** respect their parents.
3 Parents **should** also listen to their children's feelings.

In the sentences above, you will see that the writer uses *should* to give advice about the best thing to do. *Should* is a special type of verb called a **modal verb**. It is always followed by another main verb with no endings like *-s* or *-ed*. (In the examples above, the verbs *brush*, *respect*, and *listen* are main verbs that come after *should*.)

Should can also be used with *not*:

4 They think she **should not** marry him.
5 She **should not** hide her feelings.

In these sentences, *not* comes directly after *should* before the main verb.

ACTIVITY 8

Practice writing sentences with *should*.

1. Write a sentence about something you should do.

   _____

2. Write a sentence about something your teacher should do.

   _____

3. Write about something your teacher should not do.

   _____

4. Write about something a good leader should not do.

   _____

5. Write about an activity that everyone should do for good health.

   _____

Read the paragraph that follows. There are four mistakes in the use of verbs with *should*. Correct the mistakes, and review your answers with your class.

I think Binh should to tell her parents about her boyfriend. She should not lies to them. Her parents know what is the best for her, and she shoulds trust them. She should explaining how much she loves him. Her parents will understand her, and they will help her. If her boyfriend is really a good man, they will accept him.

Rewriting 1

Review your composition from Writing 1. Does the first paragraph give a summary of Binh's problem? Does the second paragraph give your opinion about what Binh should do?

Does each paragraph have a topic sentence to show its most important idea? Are all the other sentences in the paragraph about that idea? If you said "no" to any of these questions, you need to reorganize your paper.

Also, check your paper for the modal verb *should*. Did you use this verb correctly? Make changes in your paper if you need to.

You can use the checklist below to help you review the important things you want to include in your composition. Write "yes" or "no" as answers to the questions on the list.

✓CHECKLIST

Content
Did you explain Binh's problem?
Did you give your advice about Binh's problem?

Organization
Is your paper divided into two paragraphs?
Do the paragraphs each have clear topics?
Does each paragraph have a topic sentence?

Grammar
Did you form simple present tense verbs correctly?
Did you form verbs with the modal *should* correctly?

When you are finished making changes and corrections to your paper, give it to your teacher.

Reading 2: Academic Reading

This is an academic reading about ideas that social scientists say about marriage between people from different cultures.

Cross-Cultural[1] Marriage

1   Many people think it is important to marry someone from their own culture group. They believe a marriage between two people from different cultures cannot be happy because of the different values and lifestyles of the two groups. However, not all cross-cultural marriages are unhappy or less successful than other marriages. Scientists who study human behavior try to find out how these cross-cultural marriages work. These marriages can succeed even though they may need more effort than marriages within the same group.

2   Psychologists study human personality and behavior. They try to find out which personal qualities are necessary for a cross-cultural marriage to work. Anthropologists and sociologists are two types of social scientists who study group behavior. Anthropologists describe the cultures of groups around the world, including their values and the things they make. Sociologists, on the other hand, usually get their information by asking questions of large groups of people in a modern, industrial society. Then they count the answers. Sociologists want to know about the different roles[2] in a group, such as the "leader" or the "caretaker." Psychologists, anthropologists, and sociologists are all interested in couples from two different cultures who have happy marriages.

[1] *Cross-cultural* (adjective) means between different cultures.
[2] *Role* (n.) means a job, or a part, that a person has.

3 Some experts on cultural studies combine the findings[3] of psychologists, anthropologists, and sociologists to advise people who are thinking about a marriage to someone from a different culture. These experts have some suggestions. They believe special situations and personal qualities must exist for a successful cross-cultural marriage.

4 First, people in happy intercultural marriages have some special qualities. Both partners should have self-confidence. Self-confident people understand that a cultural difference in their partner's behavior is not a personal attack. Also, they should both feel a strong commitment to their marriage. They will need a lot of commitment when there are problems outside their marriage, such as the disapproval of their families.

5 Another important quality to have in an intercultural marriage is flexibility, that is, the ability to change. If both partners are flexible, they can each change their cultural habits enough to live together comfortably. They also need to be sensitive to each other's feelings, since these may be different depending on culture. For example, people in some cultures like to be alone a lot, while those in other cultures want to have people around them all the time. In a marriage between people from these two different cultures, each partner has to respect the other's need for privacy or the company of others. If not, the couple probably cannot live happily together.

6 Psychologists say that two of the most important qualities to have in a cross-cultural marriage are adventurousness and a sense of humor. Adventurous people like to try different experiences. They are not afraid of new situations. For example, they usually enjoy new foods and languages. Also, in interviews with many couples in cross-cultural marriages, they say it is important to laugh at themselves when they have a cultural misunderstanding. They advise other cross-cultural couples not to take all their misunderstandings seriously. Often the problem is between their two cultures rather than between the two of them personally.

7 In the book, *Intercultural Marriage: Promises and Pitfalls*, the author Dugan Romano says that "good motives" for getting married are necessary for the marriage to succeed. By "good motives," she means positive reasons for marriage instead of negative reasons, such as rebellion against one's culture or family. Romano feels that love "in the true sense" is the best possible reason for all marriages, including cross-cultural ones. For her, true love means not just romantic attraction, but both partners helping each other to develop.

8 In all marriages, including cross-cultural marriages, it is important for both partners to have similar goals. In some cultures, love between the two partners is not the main reason for getting married, although love may grow later. Two people may marry for security, to help their family, or for other reasons besides personal love. If both partners have the same practical reasons for marriage, their marriage can succeed. They do not have to be "in love" when they marry to be happy together.

---

[3] *Findings* (n.) are the results or the conclusions of scientists after they study something.

9 Usually partners from two cultures that are similar in values and lifestyle understand each other better than partners from extremely different cultures. For example, marriages between partners from Denmark and Norway are probably easier than marriages between partners from two very different cultures such as Denmark and Japan. However, just because two cultures are near each other does not always mean that they get along well. China and Japan are close to each other on the map, but people from those two cultures can have big cultural differences.

10 If one culture doesn't accept cross-cultural marriage, these bad feelings can affect a cross-cultural marriage. There may be prejudice against the couple and their children in that culture. The family may have negative feelings about the marriage. The family can put a lot of pressure on their family member not to marry, or to separate after marriage. Sometimes the family even refuses to see their relative or the children born into the marriage. The family member may feel lonely and sad. He or she may decide to leave the marriage and go back to the family.

11 Not many people say that cross-cultural marriages are easy, but some psychologists, sociologists, and anthropologists say these marriages can be successful. They may even be more interesting than other marriages. People who are thinking about marrying outside their culture should ask themselves if they have the personal qualities and cultural conditions to help their marriage succeed.

Vocabulary

ACTIVITY 11 Find these new words in sentences in the reading. Then put the new words in the group they belong to below, either "feelings" or "behavior."

combine (verb)	**habit** (noun)
advise (verb)	**attraction** (noun)
self-confident (adjective)	**practical** (adjective)
disapproval (noun)	**prejudice** (noun)

Feelings   **Behavior**

1. _____   1. _____

2. _____   2. _____

3. _____   3. _____

4. _____   4. _____

Academic Words Read the sample sentences below. They contain academic vocabulary from Reading 2 that might be new to you.

1. If you have a good **attitude** in your thinking about another language, it will be easier to learn.

2. Children of divorced parents are sometimes more afraid of **commitment** to a marriage than other people.

3. I enjoy the **contrasting** weather of hot summers and cold winters in my country.

4. The kind of English people speak in New York and California is **similar**, but not exactly the same.

5. A person with cancer needs the medical advice of an **expert**.

6. Young people are often more **flexible** than old people; they can change their plans more easily.

7. One of the **goals** of this book is to help students write more clearly.

8. The robber's **motives** for stealing the money were unclear because he was already rich.

9. Children need the **security** of clear rules in their lives.

Each of the sentences below has one of the academic words above. Match the beginning of each sentence with the best ending. Think about the meaning and grammar of each sentence. Write the letter of the best ending in the space at the end of the beginning.

Beginnings

1. I'm **flexible** about restaurants; _____

2. Children should have cell phones for **security** _____

3. I like the **contrasting** tastes _____

4. The daughter made a **commitment** to her mother _____

5. What are your **goals** for studying English: _____

6. The young woman's **motives** for marrying

   the rich old man _____

7. The saleswoman had a bad **attitude**

   toward customers, _____

8. Because Dr. Brown is an **expert** on flowers, _____

9. Two **similar** names in English are _____

Endings

a. "Susan" and "Suzanne."

b. to visit her once a week.

c. if they walk home from school alone.

d. he spends a lot of time in gardens.

e. so she lost a lot of business.

f. I don't care where we eat.

g. of sweet and salty food.

h. to have a better social life, or to get a better job?

i. were to use all his money.

Discussion

ACTIVITY 13 What answers does the reading give to the following questions? Answers should include what the reading says. Your own opinions and experiences might be different, but don't include them here.

1. Are cross-cultural marriages always unhappier than marriages within the same culture? Why or why not?

   _____

   _____

   _____

2. What do psychologists study?

   _____

   _____

3. What methods that sociologists use to study groups are different from the methods of anthropologists?

   _____

   _____

4. Name at least three personal qualities that this article says are necessary in a cross-cultural marriage. Explain why each quality is important.

   _____

   _____

   _____

5. What example does the reading give of possible problems in a marriage between two cultures that are near each other?

   _____

   _____

6. How can prejudice affect an intercultural marriage?

   _____

   _____

Composition Analysis

The Introduction The introductory paragraph of a composition should tell the reader the topic of the whole composition and the point or important idea about that topic. The introduction is usually the first and sometimes the second paragraph of the composition. For example, the topic may be U.S. child-raising customs, and the important point about this topic may be the importance of developing independence in children in the United States.

ACTIVITY 14 Read the introduction to Reading 2, which is the first paragraph. The topic of the introductory paragraph is the topic of the whole composition.

Write the topic of the introduction on the lines below. This is the answer to the question "What is this composition about?"

_____

_____

Paragraph 1 also tells us the main point about the topic of the composition. One of the sentences tells us the most important idea in the composition. Write the sentence in paragraph 1 that tells the main point of the composition on the lines below.

_____

_____

Writing 2

ACTIVITY 15 In the writing assignment for this part, you will write about Jack and Binh, the cross-cultural couple you already read about, and the problems in their relationship. Read about their situation, and then answer the questions that follow.

1   Jack and Binh recently decided to get married. Binh, Jack's girlfriend, told her parents about the decision, and they are very upset. They say that Binh's future husband will never be welcome in their home.

2   Binh feels very sad about their reaction. She is starting to worry that this marriage is not a good idea. She is afraid to lose her family's love and support if she marries Jack.

3   Jack feels happy about marrying Binh. His parents are glad that he found someone he loves. Most of Jack's friends congratulate him. Jack understands that marrying someone from another culture is difficult, but he believes that his relationship with Binh is strong.

4   Jack does not understand why Binh is listening to her parents' advice. Jack believes that counseling can help them decide if they can have a happy marriage. However, Binh is not interested in marriage counseling. She does not want to talk about her feelings with a stranger. Finally, Jack decides to see a marriage counselor by himself.

1. What are Jack's feelings about his situation?

_____

_____

2. What are Binh's feelings about her family situation?

_____

_____

3. Do you think it is possible for this couple to have a happy marriage or not?

_____

_____

ACTIVITY 16   **Writing Assignment** Imagine you are the marriage counselor that Jack goes to visit. You know about the ideas of psychologists, sociologists, and anthropologists on cross-cultural marriage described in Reading 1. You must write a report about your discussion with Jack.

The first paragraph of your report is an introduction that tells about the reason for Jack's visit. Write notes on the lines below about your introduction to the report. The notes should be short groups of words, not complete sentences.

_____

_____

The second paragraph describes Jack's feelings and his situation. It tells about the reactions of his family and friends. Write your notes here.

_____

_____

The third paragraph tells about Binh's feelings and her family situation. Write notes about it here.

_____

_____

In the last paragraph, you should give your conclusions about the future of this marriage. Tell about your advice to Jack. Is it possible for this couple to have a happy marriage or not? Write your notes here.

_____

_____

Now, use your notes to write a complete report of four paragraphs that describes Jack and Binh's situation and gives advice about what they should do.

Grammar

Pronouns

The following sentences begin with the same subject, *Many people*.

> Many people think it is important to marry someone from the same background. **Many people** believe a marriage between two people from different cultural groups cannot be happy …

The second sentence sounds strange, because it repeats *Many people*. We would usually use a **pronoun** (*they*), instead of *Many people*, to be the subject of the verb *believe*.

> Many people think it is important to marry someone from the same background. **They** believe a marriage between two people from different cultural groups cannot be happy …

Here are some more sentences with pronouns:

> She feels terrible about not seeing **him** anymore.
> She feels sure he loves **her**, too …
> The marriage counselor can help **them** decide what to do …

In these sentences, the writer does not want to repeat *Jack* and *Binh*, so he uses the pronouns *him*, *her*, and *them* in place of their names. Notice that in these sentences, the pronouns are direct objects of the verbs, called **object pronouns**.

Now look at the following sentences:

> Binh is afraid to tell **her** family about **her** boyfriend.
> Sociologists get **their** information by asking questions of large groups.
> The report tells about Jack's feelings and **his** situation.

All of these sentences tell about things that belong to people. They use **possessive pronouns** such as *his*, *her*, or *their* to avoid repeating the names of the people who own these things.

ACTIVITY 17 Write a pronoun to take the place of each noun (in **boldface**) in the following sentences. Sometimes you will use these subject pronouns: *he, she, it, they.* In other spaces you will need object pronouns: *him, her, it, them.* Sometimes you will need to use the possessive pronouns *her, his,* and *their* to show that something belongs to people.

Young people in the United States usually choose (1. young people's) _____ own careers. (2. Young people) _____ think that (3. young people) _____ can decide on the best career for themselves. (4. The career) _____ should be very interesting for (5. the young people) _____. The parents sometimes want (6. the parents') _____ children to do a career that is boring or too difficult for (7. their children) _____. The father may want (8. the father's) _____ son to follow the same job (9. the father) _____ does, but the son may not have any interest in (10. the same job) _____. The son often does not follow (11. the father) _____ in a career. Usually the mother hopes (12. the mother's) _____ children will find a job near home, but (13. the mother) _____ can't stop (14. the children) _____ from moving far away for a good job. They may miss (15. their mother) _____, but (16. the children's) _____ choice of career is more important. Parents in the United States do not usually try to choose a career for (17. the parents') _____ children.

ACTIVITY 18 Read the paragraph that follows. Write the correct form of a pronoun to fill in the blanks in the sentences. Review your answers with your class.

Earlier today I spoke to a young man named Jack. (1.)_____ plans to marry a woman named Binh, who is Vietnamese. (2.)_____ is worried that (3.)_____ future wife is not sure about (4.)_____ marriage. I asked Jack about the couple's relationship and I gave (5.)_____ some advice.

Binh is discussing (6.)_____ plans for marriage with (7.)_____ parents. (8.)_____ seem to be very traditional, and (9.)_____ want to approve of (10.)_____ daughter's marriage partner. (11.)_____

are against the idea of her marriage to a man outside their group.

I told Jack that (12.)_____ and Binh need to work on

(13.)_____ relationship. He needs to understand that Binh is very close to

(14.)_____ family, and their advice is important to (15.)_____. Also,

Binh needs to decide if (16.)_____ is ready to make (17.)_____ own

decision.

Rewriting 2

ACTIVITY 19

Use the checklist below to answer questions about your paper from Activity 16. If the answer is "no" to any of the questions, make changes in your paper. Pay special attention to the way you used subject, object, and possessive pronouns. When you are finished, give your paper to your teacher.

> ✓ CHECKLIST
>
> **Organization**
> Is your paper divided into paragraphs?
> Is the first paragraph an introduction to the whole report that gives its important point or main idea?
> Does each paragraph have a clear topic?
> Does each paragraph have a topic sentence that shows its important idea?
> Do you give reasons to support your opinions?
>
> **Grammar**
> Did you choose the correct tense for each verb?
> Did you use the correct endings for each verb?
> Did you use *should* with the simple form of the main verb?
> Did you use subject, object, and possessive pronouns correctly?

Internet Activities

For additional activities related to this chapter, go to elt.thomson.com/catalyst.

The Power of Murals

Exploring the Topic

Discussion Discuss these questions with a partner. Your teacher may ask you to report what you discussed.

1. Describe the photograph shown at right. What is happening in the picture? What do you feel or think about when you look at it?

2. Tell about a local person who is popular and important to the residents in your neighborhood. This person is a leader in your community, someone who makes it a better place to live or gives the residents hope for their future.

Reading 1: Personal Experience Reading

This is a reading about a large outdoor painting called a mural.

Exploring Mural Art

1   The mural on page 35 is from a part of Philadelphia, Pennsylvania, where many Spanish-speaking people live. The mural is on a wall above a community garden. There is a fence around the garden to protect it. The name of this mural, "Tribute Mural," means that the makers of this mural probably admire the famous Mexican artist, Diego Rivera. Like many of Rivera's murals, it shows pictures of people who are working in different occupations in both the city and the country. Many of the people look like they come from Latin America because of their clothes and faces.

2   The picture does not look real, like a photograph. Some figures next to each other have completely different sizes. Some of them seem to float in the air, or they seem to be in a different place from other figures in the same panel. Like Rivera's work, this mural has a simple, almost child-like style.

3   The mural has three parts, or panels. When people pass this mural on the street, they usually look at the middle part first, perhaps because it has more figures and they are a little larger than the figures in the side panels. Also, people's eyes can move up quickly from the man at the table in the middle to the woman who is carrying a basket on her head. There is tropical fruit in her basket; perhaps she is planning to sell it in the marketplace. Two men are picking mangoes from a tree to put into her basket. Below the woman is another scene; a group of people who seem to be a family are eating a meal together. A man who may be the father is sitting at the head of the table. He is breaking bread with his hands for everyone to eat. Other members of the group, including young people and an old man (maybe the grandfather) are waiting to eat the food in their bowls. Maybe it is soup or black beans from the pot on the table. Some of the group members are holding hands. Maybe they are saying a prayer of thanks for their food.

4   The section on the right shows people at work in a city, either in Latin America or the United States. Two men in work clothes are lifting a metal beam to make a skyscraper. Two other men in overalls are supervising the work. Another man is looking at a paper, which is probably a plan of the new building. On the bottom left, a man is using a hammer to hit something. At the bottom of the picture a man is holding out his arms. It looks like he is welcoming us into the mural.

5   In the left section, a woman is carrying a bunch of white lilies while a young girl, perhaps her child, is reaching up for them. Diego Rivera did a similar painting of a woman who is selling flowers in a market. On her right, a man is carrying sugar cane, perhaps after he cut it in the fields. Rivera also made a famous painting of workers who are cutting sugar cane. A tree with huge green leaves is growing behind the figures in this panel.

6   In a border on the top and the side of the mural, there are a number of small objects which are not part of the three main panels. For example, there is a starfish, a moon, and a sun with a face in it. There are two open books and several pieces of bamboo. There is also an unborn baby and a fried egg. It is hard to guess why the painters put these objects around the murals. Many of these things are part of nature everywhere, such as the sun and the moon. The starfish and bamboo are often found in warm places such as Latin America. Books like these are important for workers' education. Maybe the painters just wanted to make a pretty frame around the mural, or maybe they wanted people to ask questions about these things. You must decide for yourself about their meaning.

7   This mural gives a feeling of energy because most of the figures are working. The workers look strong and healthy, and they are doing many different jobs. Therefore, the mural shows the hard work of Latin Americans, both in their own countries and the United States. The creators of this mural probably want Latin Americans who see this mural in their neighborhood to feel pride about their people. The creators may want the mural to remind Latin Americans and others who pass it in the neighborhood that most Spanish speakers are hard-working people who contribute a lot to their new home. The large group at table together shows the importance of sharing group life for Latin Americans.

8   Because it imitates the murals of a great Mexican artist, Diego Rivera, this mural may also remind Latin Americans and others of the contributions from Latin America to the arts. It may give a feeling of respect, hope, and beauty to immigrants from Latin America in that neighborhood. A mural like this one can bring positive changes into immigrants' lives even though it is only a picture. Murals can have a powerful effect on a community.

Vocabulary

ACTIVITY 2 You may already know these words from Reading 1:

fence (noun)	**prayer** (noun)
float (verb)	**bottom** (noun)
basket (noun)	**bunch** (noun)
bowl (noun)	**border** (noun)
beans (noun)	**pride** (noun)

Choose the best word from the list to go in each space in the paragraph below. Use each word only one time. There will be two extra words you will not use.

A farmer decided to surprise his wife by cooking some fresh vegetables for their dinner. He opened the door in the _____ around his garden and went in. He felt a lot of _____ in his garden. There was a _____ of flowers around the vegetables. He cut some _____ and a _____ of carrots, and he put them in a _____. Then he took them to the kitchen and cooked them in a pot for their next meal. He put some salt and water in the _____ of the pot. Finally, he served them in a _____ on the dinner table. The farmer's wife said, "These vegetables are delicious. You're a good gardener, and a great cook, too!"

ACTIVITY 3 **Academic Words** Read the sample sentences. They contain academic vocabulary in **boldface** that might be new to you. Then, in the sentences that follow, choose the academic word from the sample sentences that fits best in each space. Review your answers with your class.

1. A **community** college should teach the people who live in its area.
2. A rich businessman should **contribute** a lot of money to his old high school.
3. The windows in the living room are made of big glass **panels** that let you look out at the mountains.
4. You should choose an **occupation** because you like the work, not simply because there are a lot of jobs in that type of work.
5. **Immigrants** who come to the United States from other countries are often very hard workers.
6. Children have a lot of **energy**; they can run and jump all day.

7. The **style** of drawing in cartoons does not look real.

8. Teachers should give a **positive** example of hard work to their students.

9. Divide your paper into four parts, and write your name in each **section**.

10. Twins look very **similar**, but not exactly the same.

a. _____ are people who move from one country to live in another one.

b. A _____ influence is good for people.

c. "_____" means "almost the same."

d. A _____ is a group of people who are the same in some way.

e. A _____ is a long piece of material.

f. You can be very active if you have a lot of _____.

g. A _____ is a part of something.

h. If people give money or time to others, they _____ a lot.

i. Your _____ is the way that you do things (especially the clothes you wear or the decoration of your house).

j. A job can also be called an _____.

Discussion

ACTIVITY 4   Discuss these questions as a class.

1. Are any changes happening in your neighborhood now? Are they good or bad changes?

2. What changes are necessary to make your neighborhood a better place to live?

Composition Analysis

Organization of a Description When you write a description of something that has different parts, whether it is a town, a car, or a mural, it is important to use some order or system as you move from one part to another.

A clear description should go in the same direction as it moves from one part to another. It can start at the top and move down, go from left to right, or right to left. Another order can be from most to least important, or least to most important. Reading 1 is an example of writing that uses a system like this.

ACTIVITY 5 Reread Reading 1, and then decide which system is used to describe the mural. Put a check next to it in the list below.

_____ a. left to right

_____ b. right to left

_____ c. top to bottom

_____ d. middle to outside

_____ e. least to most important

Writing 1

ACTIVITY 6 Look at the photograph of the mural with the title, "The History of Chinatown." It was made to celebrate the 125th anniversary of Chinatown in Philadelphia. However, many of the situations in the mural happened in Chinatowns in cities all over the United States. Study the mural and write sentences that answer the questions below.

The History of Chinatown

1. What is the name of the mural?

   _____

2. Where is this mural?

   _____

3. What is the general subject or topic of the pictures in the mural?

   _____

4. At the top of the mural, who is the largest person?

   _____

5. What is he doing? What are the other people near him doing?

   _____

   _____

6. Why did the artists put this action into the mural?

   _____

7. What is the curve at the top of the mural?

   _____

   _____

8. What does the curve change into in the middle section?

   _____

9. Who are the people in the middle part?

   _____

10. Where are they?

    _____

11. What are the people in the middle section doing?

    _____

    _____

12. What other important things are in this scene?

    _____

    _____

13. What form does the curve change into in the bottom section?

_____

14. What is the meaning of the large hand and the bulldozer in the bottom part?

_____

15. What are the man and boy doing?

_____

16. Where are the children at the end of the curve?

_____

17. What are these children doing?

_____

18. As you follow the curve, what story does the mural tell about the history of Chinese immigrants to the United States?

_____

_____

19. What feelings do you get from the different parts of this mural?

_____

_____

20. What do the Chinese immigrants' experiences make you feel about your own experiences here?

_____

_____

21. What ideas do you think the designers of this mural want people to get from it?

_____

_____

ACTIVITY 7 **Writing Assignment** Write a composition to describe "The History of Chinatown" mural. Review the answers you wrote to the questions in Activity 6 above. You can use the outline below to help you plan your paper. Group your answers to the questions into paragraphs to describe the different parts of the mural and your reaction to it.

> **Introduction:** General information about the mural
>
> **First body paragraph:** description of the top of the mural
>
> **Second body paragraph:** description of the middle of the mural
>
> **Third body paragraph:** description of the bottom of the mural
>
> **Conclusion:** the feeling you have about the mural; ideas you have about the meaning of the mural

When you are finished, put your paper aside for a while.

Grammar

Present Progressive Verb Tense

Here are some sentences from the mural description that use the present progressive verb tense:

1 Two men **are picking** mangoes from a tree.
2 Some of the group members **are holding** hands.
3 He **is breaking** bread with his hands.
4 A tree with huge green leaves **is growing** behind the figures in this panel.

Sentences with verbs in the present progressive tense tell about the actions that are happening now, such as the activities in the mural while we are looking at them. Sometimes "now" can include a longer period of time like "today," or "this afternoon," "this week," or even "this year." We can use the present progressive verb tense to express activities that are going on at the present time.

In the example sentences above, notice that a form of the verb *be* comes between the subject and the main verb. This verb has different forms (*is, are, am*) in different sentences. The form of *be* must agree with its subject. You must put a form of *be* after the subject when you write in the present progressive tense. This shows the present time. Then put the main verb with *-ing* after it.

Subject	*be*	Main Verb	
He	is	breaking	bread with his hands.
Two men	are	picking	mangoes from a tree.
I	am	counting	the people with glasses in this room.

The negative form of the present progressive tense is made the same way as the negative form of the verb *be* alone. That is, you put *not* between the form of *be* and the main verb with *-ing*. For example,

You are **not** studying Chinese in this class.

Write a sentence about the activities that each of these people in your school are doing right now. Use the present progressive tense.

1. The interested students _____

_____

2. The bored students _____

_____

3. My teacher _____

_____

4. The leader (president or principal) of my school _____

_____

5. The secretaries in their offices _____

_____

ACTIVITY 9

Write a sentence about each of the following people to tell what they are **not** doing now. Use the **negative form** of the present progressive tense.

1. The leader of my country _____

_____

2. The students in this class _____

_____

3. My best friend and I _____

_____

4. I _____

_____

5. You (the student next to you) _____

_____

Rewriting 1

ACTIVITY 10   Check all the verbs in your Writing 1 composition about the mural, "The History of Chinatown." Underline the subject of each sentence. For every verb in the present progressive tense, check that there is a *be* verb in the correct form (*is*, *are*, *am*) that agrees with its subject. Then find the main verb and check that it has *-ing* at the end.

ACTIVITY 11   Review your composition from Writing 1.

Does each paragraph have a topic sentence to show its most important idea? Are all the other sentences in the paragraph about that idea? If you said "no" to any of these questions, you need to reorganize your paper.

You can use the checklist below to help you review the other important things you want to include in your composition. Write "yes" or "no" as answers to the questions on the list.

> **CHECKLIST**
>
> **Content**
> Did you describe each part of the mural?
> Did you describe your feelings and ideas about the mural?
>
> **Organization**
> Is your paper divided into paragraphs?
> Does each paragraph have a clear topic and a topic sentence?
>
> **Grammar**
> Did you form present progressive tense verbs correctly?

When you are finished making corrections to your paper, give it to your teacher.

Reading 2: Academic Reading

This is an academic reading about the history of murals in the United States.

History of the Mural Movement

1   The mural movement started in Mexico in the 1920s, when the Mexican government asked famous Mexican artists such as Diego Rivera, José Orozco, and David Siqueiros to paint murals about national history and culture. These artists made their murals on the walls of public buildings such as schools and government offices.

2   Perhaps because it has many residents with families from Mexico, Los Angeles, California, was the first city in the United States that had a lot of murals. In the 1960s and 70s, both artists and neighborhood residents made murals. These murals expressed their experiences and concerns. The mural arts movement has continued in Los Angeles from those days until the present time. Many Los Angeles residents now are immigrants from Latin America, Asia, and other parts of the world. A lot of murals in Los Angeles today express the feelings, ideas, and dreams of their communities' residents, including the immigrants there.

Murals in the United States Today

3   These days the number of murals is increasing in both large and small cities in the United States. The murals can bring beauty to areas that are poor and run-down because the residents do not have enough money to fix their houses. There are also a lot of abandoned buildings in poor neighborhoods that look bad, but they have good walls for murals. Often the murals are about local heroes and history or peaceful landscapes. Sometimes the artists include the faces of real people from the neighborhood in their murals.

The Process of Making a Mural

4   A mural project often begins when artists teach young neighborhood people about making murals. These students help the artists to paint murals. The students feel excited and proud because they are helping to create beautiful murals that improve their neighborhoods. Some of the students become professional artists themselves later. The other residents of the neighborhood also feel more positive about the community because it looks better. Not many people write graffiti on the murals or leave trash in front of them.

5   Philadelphia, Pennsylvania, is another city in the United States with a very large number of murals. Its present-day Mural Arts Program started in the 1980s as a way to get young graffiti artists to use their talents in more positive ways. The city government gets professional artists to plan a mural after talking to the neighbors to find out their ideas for it. Many Philadelphia residents are immigrants from all over the world, especially from China, the Caribbean, Africa, and eastern Europe. Because they participate in the plans, the murals can bring them closer to other residents in the neighborhood who were born in the United States. They get to know each other more through the mural projects, and little by little, they may understand each other better. Immigrants can feel like part of the community when their ideas and concerns are in a neighborhood mural.

6   San Francisco, California, and Chicago, Illinois, are other major cities that have active mural programs. These two cities have some of the same urban situations. They both have a lot of immigrants from other countries who can express their feelings about their lives in murals.

7   The murals in both big and small cities all over the United States often recognize immigrant people's backgrounds, their difficulties, their contributions to their new country, and their successes. Non-immigrant people in these cities may become more aware of immigrants' lives through the content of murals. They can understand immigrants better and appreciate them more.

Vocabulary

ACTIVITY 12 You probably already know the words below from Reading 2. To check your understanding of these words, choose one of them to complete each of the sentences below. Use each word only one time. There will be two extra words. After you are done, review your answers with your class.

movement (noun)	**increasing** (verb)	**program** (noun)
government (noun)	**local** (adjective)	**especially** (adverb)
express (verb)	**excited** (adjective)	**situation** (noun)
concern (noun)	**improve** (verb)	**background** (noun)

1. Nobody likes to be in an unhappy _____.

2. In a family photograph, the parents are usually behind their children in the _____.

3. The _____ of the United States is in Washington, D.C.

4. A good way to _____ your spelling is to read a lot.

5. Grandparents are usually very _____ about their first grandchild.

6. Most children like to go to a _____ school where they can see their friends from the neighborhood.

7. The number of people in the world with AIDS is _____ very fast.

8. Many cities in the United States have a _____ to help old people with shopping and meals.

9. People _____ their opinions when they vote.

10. It is _____ hard to speak another language when you are tired.

ACTIVITY 13 **Academic Words** Read the following sentences. They show the meanings of the academic words in **boldface**.

1. It is dangerous to go into an **abandoned** house where nobody lives.

2. I **appreciate** your kindness; you helped me a lot!

3. I wasn't **aware** that we need to pay for our books—nobody told me.

4. The old part of the city is a dangerous **area**.

5. A good writer can **create** a story that seems real, although it is not.

6. Everyone should **participate** in our neighborhood cleanup to make our street look better.

7. If you have a problem with your back, you should get **professional** help from a doctor.

8. Learning a new language is not a fast **process** for most people; it has many steps.

9. The **residents** of the apartment building complained about the dirty building.

Match the number of the academic word with the letter of its meaning.

1. _____ abandoned
2. _____ appreciate
3. _____ be aware of
4. _____ area
5. _____ create
6. _____ participate
7. _____ professional
8. _____ process
9. _____ resident

a. part of a place
b. make something new
c. action that happens step by step
d. person who lives in a place
e. know about something
f. be thankful for something
g. not lived in
h. having special training, related to work
i. be part of an action

Discussion

ACTIVITY 14   Choose two or three of the following topics to discuss with a partner.

1. What information do you think people from other cultures in the United States should know about your country of birth?

2. Are there many new immigrants to the United States now from your country? Why or why not?

3. How do you express your feelings and ideas—by making art, by making or listening to music, by writing, or in some other way?

4. Do you know some of your neighbors? Why or why not?

Composition Analysis

The Conclusion The last paragraph of a composition is its **conclusion**. It shows that the writer's presentation is coming to an end. In the conclusion, the important point or main idea of the whole composition can be repeated with different words to make the readers remember it. In addition, the writer may want to add one last thought about that main idea. The writer may talk about the future, express a wish about the idea, or go from that specific idea to a more general idea. Whatever type of conclusion the writer chooses, it should give the readers the feeling of an ending. Readers should not feel like they are still waiting for something more.

ACTIVITY 15 Review Reading 2 and read the conclusion carefully. Check the methods in the list below that the writer of this conclusion uses to bring the composition to an end. More than one method may be used to finish the composition.

_____ 1. Talks about the main idea in the future

_____ 2. Expresses a wish about this idea

_____ 3. Goes from a specific idea to a general idea

Writing 2

ACTIVITY 16 A memorandum or "memo" is one of the formal ways of communicating in writing. A memo is like a short letter. It should be easy to read quickly. It begins with the heading "Memorandum" in the center. It also includes lines at the top that give basic information about who is writing, whom they are writing to, why they are writing, and the date. The heading of a memo looks like this:

MEMORANDUM

TO: Judith Hay

FROM: Jack Straw

SUBJECT: Proposal on holidays

Date: May 30, 2010

Write a short memo to your teacher. Tell your teacher about one suggestion you have for making an improvement in your class. Your suggestion might be about homework, tests, classroom work, your textbook, or other topics related to your class.

ACTIVITY 17 **Writing Assignment** In this writing assignment, you will write a proposal for a mural project for your own neighborhood. A proposal is a written plan to do something new. You will imagine that you and a group of neighbors are planning the mural and you have decided to ask a mural program to help you pay for paint and other expenses.

Begin your mural project by drawing the basic parts of the mural. It does not matter if you are not good at drawing. Your drawing only shows the parts of your mural and where they will be placed. Your drawing should include the people, objects, or animals that will be in the mural. It should show what the people or animals are doing. When you are finished with your drawing, use it to help you with your writing.

Now write a proposal for this mural. When you write, imagine that you and a group of neighbors are planning a mural for your own neighborhood. Your group is writing to a mural arts program for help with your plan. You need to tell the mural arts program about the importance of your mural to your neighborhood.

Your proposal should be in the form of a memorandum or "memo." Begin your proposal using the form below, which includes the person or group you are writing to, your name, and the topic or subject you are writing about.

MEMORANDUM

TO: Mural Arts Program

FROM: (your name)

SUBJECT: (write the name of your mural with one or several words, not a sentence)

DATE: (the date)

In your introductory paragraph, write about the subject of your mural. Describe the subject that you and your neighbors have chosen. Explain why you are writing to the program (for help with your expenses) and what you would like them to do.

In the second, and possibly third paragraph (if you have a lot of ideas), write a detailed description of the people, actions, and things you want to have in your mural. As in the description of the "Tribute Mural," use some kind of system or order for your description (left to right, top to bottom, etc.) What figures are there in the mural, and what is each of them doing? What other important things are in the mural? Does your mural show more than one situation? If so, use an order to describe each of the scenes.

In your conclusion (final paragraph), write about the ideas and feelings you want to present through these figures, actions, and objects in your mural. What reactions do you hope to get from the people passing by, both from your neighbors and other people?

Grammar

Modal Verbs *can,* *may,* **and** *should*

Look at these sentences from Reading 2.

1 The murals **can** bring beauty to areas that are poor.
2 Immigrants **can** feel like part of the community.
3 They **can** understand immigrants better.
4 Little by little, they **may** understand each other better.
5 Non-immigrant people in these cities **may** become more aware of immigrants' lives.

You learned about the modal verb *should* in Chapter 2. A modal verb tells something about the way the main verb is done. After the modal verb, its main verb has no endings such as *-ed, -s,* or *-ing.*

Both of the modal verbs *can* and *may* have several meanings. In this reading, the modal *may* shows that the writer thinks the action or event is possible, but it is not completely sure. For example,

Non-immigrant people in these cities **may** become more aware of immigrants' lives.

Some of the non-immigrants will become more aware, and some will not. It is not a definite action.

The modal *can* adds a different meaning to the main verb: it shows that the subject is able to do that action. For example,

The murals **can** bring beauty to areas that are poor.

In this sentence, *can* means that the murals are able to bring beauty to these areas.

You saw in Chapter 2 that *should* is used with *not* to make negative sentences. Notice that *not* also follows *can* and *may* in negative sentences.

6 Immigrants **may not** feel part of the communities around them.
7 The project **cannot** continue without help from the neighbors.

In these sentences, *not* comes after *can* and *may.* Notice that *cannot,* the negative form of *can,* is spelled as one word.

A. Write three sentences about an action that **may** happen in the future, but it is not certain. The first one is done as an example.

1. _I may go to a baseball game if it doesn't rain._

2. _____

3. _____

4. _____

B. Now write three sentences about an action someone **can** do, meaning someone "is able to" do it.

1. _My friend can speak five languages._

2. _____

3. _____

4. _____

Find four errors in the use of the negative forms of *can* and *may* in the following paragraph.

It is very important to think positively about learning another language. You will probably learn a lot faster if you avoid thoughts like, "I can not learn this grammar—it's too confusing!" If you think to yourself, "The spelling in this language is crazy—I not can remember all the rules," you may not learning to spell very quickly. Your progress may not be fast because you are stopping your own learning. Instead, tell yourself, "These rules can't stopped me from learning the language! I *will* succeed!"

Rewriting 2

ACTIVITY 20 Use the checklist below to make sure your writing assignment from Activity 17 is correct. If the answer is "no" to any of these questions, make corrections in your paper. When you are finished, give your paper to your teacher.

CHECKLIST

Content

Does your proposal give an exciting plan for your mural that will interest some people in giving time and money for it?

Organization

Is your proposal divided into paragraphs?

Does each paragraph have a clear topic?

Does each paragraph have a topic sentence at or near the beginning?

Do the paragraphs describing the mural move from one section to another with an order or system (for example, "left to right" or "important to less important")?

Does the conclusion (paragraph at the end of your proposal) repeat the important idea for the mural and give one last comment about it?

Does your proposal sound like it is finished at the end, or does it leave the reader waiting for more?

Grammar

Did you use the correct verb tense for each verb?

Did you use the present progressive verb tense to show actions that are happening now in the mural?

Did you always use the modals *can* and *may* with the base form of their main verbs?

Did you use the modals *can* and *may* with their correct meanings?

Internet Activities

For additional activities related to this chapter, go to elt.thomson.com/catalyst.

New Life for Cities

Exploring the Topic

Discussion Discuss your neighborhood with your class.

1. Describe the buildings and the people. Are the buildings new, old, or both? How tall are they? What are they made of? What is the nationality of most people in your neighborhood—are they from the United States or other countries? Are most people young, old, or different ages? What kind of work do people do?

2. Tell what you know about the history of your neighborhood. Do you know when the buildings were built? Do you know who lived in your neighborhood in the past?

3. Discuss how you feel about your neighborhood. Is it a good place to live? Are the neighbors friendly and helpful? Is it quiet or busy? Is it safe?

Reading 1: Personal Experience Reading

The following story is about a family that lives in a city neighborhood. The family plans to make a new home in an old neighborhood. When you read this story, think about ideas that can help them with their plans.

Greenwood Returns to Life

1   There is an old neighborhood in the city called Greenwood. In the past, this neighborhood was in an industrial area. Then, the businesses moved away, and many people also moved away. Many homes and other buildings became empty. Greenwood was dying.

2   A few years ago, people started to move into Greenwood again. Many of these people were immigrants. Some new people bought old buildings and fixed them. Some people bought empty houses that no one wanted. They fixed them and began to live in them. Some of these new people started new businesses, such as stores and restaurants. Now, Greenwood is alive again.

3   There is a new family in Greenwood, the Patels. They live in an apartment on Division Street, at number 664. They want to buy the house next door, at number 662. The house is empty. The owners moved away last year, and no one lives there now. The Patels want to borrow money from a bank in the community, buy the house, and repair it. They plan to fix the roof and walls

and paint the house. They plan to put electricity into the house and fix the water pipes. All of this work will cost money.

4   A few months ago the Patels applied to the bank for a loan. They wanted to borrow the money to buy the house and to repair it. The cost is very low, only $10,000. The other plans for the house, the roof, the walls, the electricity, and the pipes, will cost about $60,000. The Patel family asked to borrow $70,000 from the bank.

5   Last week a loan officer from the bank wrote a letter to the Patels. The loan officer said that the bank would not give a loan to the family to buy 662 Division Street. He gave three reasons for the decision.

6   First, the loan officer said the bank could not loan so much money for that house. Even after the repairs, the house will only be worth $50,000. That is how much people pay for similar houses in the neighborhood.

7   Second, the bank cannot make a loan to the Patels because the family never borrowed money from a bank before. The bank could not be sure that the Patels will be able to pay back the loan on time.

8   Third, the income of the Patel family is too low. Only the father works, and the family's income is about $30,000 a year. The bank says that is not enough to pay back the loan.

9   The Patel family had a meeting one evening to discuss the letter from the bank. The father decided to write back to the loan officer and ask again for the loan. He asked the oldest daughter, Bela, to write the letter. The whole family gave their ideas about what to write in the letter.

Vocabulary

ACTIVITY 2   You probably already know the words below. To check your understanding of these words, choose one of the words to fit in each sentence. After you are done, review your answers with your class.

empty (adjective)	**pipe** (noun)
borrow (verb)	**loan** (here a noun, also a verb)
roof (noun)	**repairs** (noun)

1. No one lived in the house. It was _____.

2. The _____ carried the rainwater into the river.

3. The bank will only give people a _____ if they can pay back the money.

4. The rain came into the house through a hole in the _____.

5. They needed to pay for the _____ to the broken door.

6. The family needs to _____ some money, but they plan to pay it back.

Academic Words Read the sample sentences. They contain academic vocabulary in **boldface** that might be new to you. Then, in the sentences that follow, choose the academic word that fits best in each sentence. Review your answers with your class.

1. A **community** is a group of people who live, work, or do other things together.

2. **Immigrants** move to a new country to live there for a long time.

3. **Income** is the amount of money that a person earns.

a. People with college degrees usually have a higher _____ than people who just finished high school.

b. In the early 1900s, there were many _____ who moved from Europe to the United States.

c. People who come from the same country often live near each other in the same _____.

Discussion

ACTIVITY 4   Discuss these questions with your classmates.

1. What do you think will happen next to the Patels?

2. What will the Patels say in the letter to the bank?

3. Do you think the bank should loan the money to the Patels? Why or why not?

Composition Analysis

Narration Reading 1 is an example of a **narration**. A narration is a composition about events, or things that happen. The paragraphs in a narration are about the different parts of a story. The topic of each paragraph is one part of the story.

ACTIVITY 5   Reading 1 has nine paragraphs. Each paragraph has a topic. The list below describes the topics of some of the paragraphs. Write the number of the paragraph that matches each of these topics.

a. The bank's letter to the Patels about the loan   Paragraph _____

b. The family's discussion about the letter from the bank   Paragraph _____

c. How Greenwood started to die   Paragraph _____

d. The problem with the family's income   Paragraph _____

e. The Patels' plans for a new house   Paragraph _____

f. How Greenwood started to live again   Paragraph _____

Discuss your answers with your class.

Writing 1

ACTIVITY 6 Work with a partner. Discuss the bank's decision not to loan money to the Patels. Include your opinion about the three points in the letter from the loan officer. Use this chart to write your ideas:

The bank says:	You say:
The house will not be worth $70,000 even after the repairs are finished.	
The bank does not know if the family will pay the loan on time.	
The income of the family is too low to pay the loan.	

ACTIVITY 7 **Writing Assignment** Write a composition about the Patels and their plans to buy and repair the house on Division Street. Write a short summary of the plans that the Patels have. Explain why the bank should (or should not) loan the money for the house to the family. You can use some of the ideas from Activity 6 above, from your class discussions, or from the reading.

You can begin your composition like this:

The Patel family lives in Greenwood. They want to buy a house in the neighborhood ...

Grammar

Simple Past Tense

Look at these sentences from the reading. All of these sentences from the story of the Patels tell about things that happened in the past. The verbs in these sentences are in the **simple past tense**.

> This neighborhood **was** in an industrial area.
> The businesses **moved** away.
> Many homes and other buildings **became** empty.
> People **started** to move into Greenwood again.
> Many of these people **were** immigrants.
> Some new people **bought** old buildings and fixed them.
> The owners **moved** away last year.
> The Patels **applied** to the bank for a loan.
> They **wanted** to borrow the money to buy the house.
> A loan officer from the bank **wrote** a letter to the Patels.
> The loan officer **said** that the bank would not give a loan to the family.
> The family never **borrowed** money from a bank before.
> The Patel family **had** a meeting.
> The father **decided** to write back to the loan officer.
> He **asked** the oldest daughter to write the letter.
> The whole family **gave** their ideas about what to write.

There are two ways to show that English verbs are in the simple past tense. One way is to add *-ed* or *-d* to the end of verbs. This is the way to form the past tense of verbs such as:

Present	Past
start	started
move	moved
apply	applied
want	wanted
borrow	borrowed
decide	decided
ask	asked

These verbs are called "regular" because there is a simple rule for forming them. Notice that the spelling of *applied* uses the letter *i* instead of *y* when you add *-ed*.

The second way to form the simple past tense is to make other changes in the verb. Because there is no simple rule for these verbs, they are called "irregular." These are the irregular verbs that you saw in the reading:

Present	Past
is	was
are	were
become	became
buy	bought
write	wrote
give	gave
say	said

Practice writing sentences in the past tense. Use Appendix 2, a dictionary, or a grammar book to find the past tense forms of irregular verbs. Write sentences to answer these questions.

1. What time did you get up today?

   _____

2. What was the last thing you did yesterday?

   _____

3. Where did you go when you left your house today?

   _____

4. What was the first thing you did when you came to class today?

   _____

5. Who was the last person you called on the telephone?

   _____

6. What did you buy the last time you went to a store?

   _____

7. When was the last time you were sick? What sickness did you have?

   _____

   _____

8. Did you teach someone how to do something in your life? What did you teach them?

   _____

   _____

Review the sentences you wrote with your teacher.

The paragraph below has some mistakes in simple past tense verb forms. Find the mistakes and make corrections. (You should find five mistakes). Discuss your answers with your class.

A few months ago the Patels ask the bank for a loan. They asked to borrow $70,000 from the bank. Last week a loan officer from the bank writed a letter to the Patels. He sayed that the bank would not give a loan to the family to buy 662 Division Street. He gaved three reasons for the decision. They were unhappy about his letter, but they decides to ask him again for the loan.

Rewriting 1

ACTIVITY 10

Use this checklist to review the changes you need to make in your paper from Activity 7. After you answer the questions, rewrite the composition you wrote about the Patels.

CHECKLIST

Content

Did you describe the plans that the Patels have for the new house?

Did you explain the reasons the bank should, or should not, loan the money to the Patels?

Organization

Is your paper divided into paragraphs?

Do the paragraphs have clear topics?

Do the paragraphs have a topic sentence?

Grammar

Did you choose the correct verb tense for each verb?

Did you use the correct forms for simple present and simple past tense verbs?

Reading 2: Academic Reading

This is an academic reading about the history of immigration in the United States.

Immigrants and Their Neighborhoods, 1840 to 2010
The Story of the Eastern Cities

1   The United States is called "a nation of immigrants." When immigrants come to this country, they usually come to the cities. In the city, they can find jobs and a place to live. Many immigrants come to the cities on the east coast of the United States. Immigrants have a big effect on life in these cities.

The 1700s and 1800s

2   In the 1700s and the early 1800s, most of the immigrants to the United States were from England, Ireland, or Germany. In the 1880s, after the Civil War, the eastern cities had many immigrants from other parts of Europe. They came from central Europe (from countries such as Poland and Hungary), from eastern Europe (from Russia and other countries), and from southern Europe (mostly from Italy and Greece). At that time, most immigrants came to the big cities in the East. The biggest city was New York. The second biggest was Philadelphia.

The 1900s and 1910s

3   The United States had its largest amount of immigration around 1910. Most immigrants at this time were poor. They lived in neighborhoods close to the center of the city. People of the same nationality usually lived together in ethnic neighborhoods. They helped each other find jobs. They often followed the same religion. They also spoke the same language. All of this made life easier for the new immigrants. Some of the ethnic neighborhoods were Italian, Jewish, Chinese, and Greek. The children of immigrants who lived in these neighborhoods learned English very well, but many older people spoke their own languages.

4   In the early 1900s, people who had more money lived outside the center of the city. These neighborhoods were sometimes called "streetcar" neighborhoods. People took streetcars into the center of the city to work, and they went home the same way. People in these neighborhoods had bigger houses, and the streets had trees on them. Immigrants did not usually live in streetcar neighborhoods.

The 1920s

5   In the 1920s, there was very little immigration to the United States. The U.S. government changed its laws. The government did not allow many new people to come from other countries. During this period, immigrants stayed in ethnic neighborhoods, but they started to change their old culture. They spoke and lived like the English-speaking people around them. There were not many new immigrants, and there were not many people who kept their old cultures.

6   In the 1920s, many immigrants in poor city neighborhoods shopped on the street. They bought fresh food every day, because they did not have a good way to keep food cool. People who sell things on the street are called street vendors. There are still street vendors in some cities today.

7   Some new people moved into eastern cities in the 1920s. Most of them were not immigrants from other countries. They were African Americans from the southern United States. Black people left the South because they felt more freedom in the North. Black Americans could find better jobs in the industrial areas in the North. They felt that they had better opportunities in northern cities such as Chicago, New York, or Philadelphia.

8   The big cities had many industries in the 1920s. The cities had old industries that built trains and ships. There were many old factories where people made leather from animal skins and cloth from wool. The cities also had newer industries, such as those that made radios.

9   Some people earned good salaries in the 1920s. Many of these people moved away from the center of the city. Some people built big houses in new neighborhoods, and some moved into the old streetcar neighborhoods. Most people who lived in these areas worked in the city. They had enough money to buy a car. They could drive to work in their cars.

The 1930s

10   When many people lose their jobs and many businesses close, it is called a "depression." In the 1930s, there was a depression in the whole world. The

1930s were bad years for most people in the cities. Many older businesses closed, and many people lost their jobs.

11   Immigrants had more problems than most native-born people in the 1930s. Many people lost their homes because they lost their jobs. People tried to help each other. They started groups that helped with food or money. Many people in industrial neighborhoods joined unions. The unions fought for higher pay.

The 1940s

12   In the1940s, many of the men and some of the women of the United States went to war. They fought in World War II. They fought in Europe and in the Pacific Ocean, against Germany, Italy, and Japan. Many of these people were immigrants or the children of immigrants.

13   In the 1940s, the government spent money on weapons, airplanes, and other machines to fight the war. People found jobs in the factories that made things for the war. This helped to end the depression.

The 1950s

14   In the 1950s, there were big changes in the United States. The war was over, and the depression was over. Men came home from the war and got new jobs. Many people wanted to have families.

15   In the 1950s, many towns outside the cities grew. People who had more money wanted to move away from the city. They wanted to live in bigger, single houses that were made for one family. They wanted a quieter life. Towns outside of a city, with bigger houses and a quieter life, are called "suburbs." People in the suburbs usually work in the city and come home to the suburbs at night.

16   The cities also changed. Children and grandchildren of immigrants built new houses in neighborhoods on the edge of the cities. The new city neighborhoods grew, and often the rest of the city's population in the center became smaller. Many families stayed in the city, but moved to new neighborhoods. When people moved to a new neighborhood, they often moved with people from the same group. People bought bigger houses. Most people still worked near home.

17   Segregation is the separation of groups of people in society. Segregation increased in the 1950s. For example, more black people moved into the cities, and many white people moved out to the suburbs. White people and black people did not usually live in the same neighborhood.

From the 1960s to the Present

18   Many things changed in the eastern cities after 1960. More industries left, and new businesses, such as banks and restaurants, opened. More immigrants came in the 1970s, 80s, and 90s. More native-born people left the city to live in the suburbs.

19   The eastern cities today still show their history. There are buildings from the 1900s, 1800s, 1700s, and sometimes the 1600s. Also, many people still live in ethnic neighborhoods.

20   Now some people are moving back to the city from the suburbs. They like the interesting life in the city, and they do not have to spend time and money

driving to work. New groups are still coming to the city, and they are still trying to make a good life there. Immigrants are important in the new life of cities all over the United States. Newspapers report that immigrants are rebuilding homes and businesses in Brooklyn, New York; Seattle, Washington; Dallas, Texas; Atlanta, Georgia; and other cities. This rebuilding is helping to keep the cities alive.

Vocabulary

ACTIVITY 11

You probably already know the words below. To check your understanding of these words, choose one of the words to fit in each sentence. After you are done, review your answers with your class.

government (noun)	**salaries** (noun)
leather (noun)	**edge** (noun)

1. The newer homes were on the _____ of the city, where there was more land.

2. Higher _____ could pay for bigger homes.

3. People used _____ to make furniture and shoes.

4. The _____ made new laws about immigrants.

ACTIVITY 12

Academic Words Read the sample sentences. They contain academic vocabulary in **boldface** that might be new to you. Then choose the academic word that fits best in the sentences (a–d) that follow. Review your answers with your class.

1. People who move from one country to another country are **immigrants**. When they move, they **immigrate** to a new country. All of this movement is called **immigration**.

2. An **ethnic** group is a group of people with the same nationality or culture.

3. **Culture** is all of the ideas, things, and ways to do things that people share in a group.

4. When people don't have money to buy things, and business stops growing, it is called a **depression**. People can also be **depressed**. It means that they do not feel good about life.

a. When the _____ was over, more people found jobs.

b. Workers from China created _____ neighborhoods in many big cities.

c. Language is one of the important parts of _____.

d. _____ from Mexico brings a lot of hard workers to U.S. businesses.

Composition Analysis

Scanning and Skimming for Topics and Ideas Good readers use several different skills when they read. One of those skills is called "skimming." **Skimming** means reading a text quickly to understand its main topics. Skimming is used to understand a text in a general way before reading carefully to understand the details. Readers often can get information about the topics in an academic reading by looking at the headings, or titles, of the different sections. For example, one of the first sections in Reading 2 has the heading "1900s and 1910s." This heading tells us that the following paragraphs are about that time period.

Sometimes we can skim a reading by looking at the topic sentences of its paragraphs. For instance, in paragraph 3 in Reading 2 the first sentence says "The United States had its largest amount of immigration around 1910." The first sentence of paragraph 4 says "People who had more money lived outside the center of the city." These two topic sentences can give us an idea of the main point of the paragraphs.

Another reading skill is called "scanning." **Scanning** means looking for specific information without reading all of the information carefully. Readers may need to scan an academic reading for a date, a fact, an example, and so on, by quickly moving their eyes over the section that has the information they need.

ACTIVITY 13 **Skim** Reading 2. Read the title of the reading and the headings for each of the sections. Read the first sentence of each paragraph. Then read the questions below. Return to the reading, and **scan** it for the information you need to answer the questions. Make a note of the paragraph number (or numbers) where you found the answers, then write answers to the questions. When you are finished, discuss the questions with your class.

1. The reading says that many immigrants who came to the United States came to the big cities. According to the reading, why did immigrants come to the cities?

   Paragraph(s): _____

   _____

   _____

2. In the early 1900s, immigrants lived in ethnic neighborhoods. What were the reasons?

   Paragraph: _____

   _____

   _____

3. Why did people buy their food in the street in the 1920s?

   Paragraph: _____

   _____

   _____

4. Many black families moved to northern and eastern cities in the 1920s. Why did this happen?

   Paragraph: _____

   _____

   _____

5. In the 1930s, the cities were in a depression. How did the depression affect the immigrants' lives?

   Paragraph: _____

   _____

   _____

6. In the 1950s, many cities came back to life after the depression. What things changed in the cities? What things stayed the same?

   Paragraph: _____

   _____

   _____

7. Of course, some things in cities today are different from cities one hundred years ago, but some things are the same. What things are different and what things are the same in cities today?

   Paragraph: _____

   _____

   _____

Writing 2

In this section you will write a composition about the people and the buildings of your neighborhood. Begin by writing answers to these questions.

Who lives in your neighborhood?

1. What is the nationality of your neighbors? If they were born in the United States, where did their parents or grandparents come from?

_____

_____

2. What kind of work do your neighbors do?

_____

_____

What do the buildings in your neighborhood look like?

3. How big are the buildings?

_____

_____

4. What are the buildings made of?

_____

_____

5. How old do you think the buildings are?

_____

_____

What do you think your neighborhood was like in the past?

6. Do you know the nationality of the people who lived in your neighborhood in the past? (If you don't know, you might ask some old people in the neighborhood.)

_____

_____

7. What kind of work did the people do?

_____

_____

8. Do you think the people who live in your neighborhood now will stay for a
    long time?

    _____

    _____

9. Will the neighborhood change? How will it change?

    _____

    _____

ACTIVITY 15 **Writing Assignment** Write a composition about the people and the buildings
of your neighborhood. Each paragraph in your composition should have its
own topic. You should have a paragraph about each of the topics below:

Who lives in your neighborhood?

What do the buildings in your neighborhood look like?

What do you think your neighborhood was like in the past?

What will be the future of your neighborhood?

You can use your answers from Activity 14 above as part of the content for
your paper. When you are finished, put your paper aside.

Grammar

Many, some, more, most Words such as *many*, *some*, *more*, and *most* are used before nouns to describe the
quantity or amount of something. Reading 2 contains examples of these words,
which you can see in these sentences:

Many immigrants come to the cities.
Many older people spoke their own languages.
The big cities had **many industries** in the 1920s.

In these sentences, *many* occurs before plural nouns, such as *immigrants* or
industries. Sometimes there can be an adjective, like *older*, before the noun.
Many can come before any plural noun, such as *people*, *families*, or *things*. This
noun can be the subject of the sentence. For example:

Many people moved away from the center of the city.
Many families stayed in the city, but moved to new neighborhoods.
Many things changed in the cities after 1960.

The noun with *many* can also be the direct object of the sentence:

The United States had **many immigrants**.
The government did not allow **many new people** to come from other
        countries.

When writers use *many* in these examples, it means that the number of immigrants, people, industries, families, etc. is large or important.

Writers also use *some* before nouns:

Some people are moving back to the city.
Some new people moved into eastern cities in the 1920s.

In these examples, the number of people is smaller than the number described by *many*. We use *some* to describe less than half of a group.

When writers use *more*, they are making a comparison between two things or people, two times, two places, etc., to show that one is larger than the other. For example:

More industries left.
More immigrants came in the 1970s, 80s, and 90s.
Immigrants had **more problems**.

Writers use *most* before nouns to describe more than half of a group:

Most immigrants came to the big cities.
Most people worked in the city.
Most children of immigrants did not move to the suburbs.

It is very common to see the words *of the* following *many*, *some*, *more*, and *most*. Here are some examples:

Most of the immigrants came to the big cities.
Some of the people do not have jobs.

ACTIVITY 16   Write sentences using *many, some, more,* and *most* that describe each of the groups below. The first one is done for you.

1. Your family members

   Some of my brothers and sisters go to college.

2. Your classmates

   _____

3. People who live in your neighborhood

   _____

4. The buildings in the neighborhood where you live

   _____

5. Immigrants to the United States

   _____

ACTIVITY 17   Look at the set of shapes below. The shapes are circles and squares. Use *some* or *most* to complete the sentences that describe this set of shapes.

1. _____ of the shapes are squares.

2. _____ of the shapes are circles.

3. _____ of the circles are white.

4. _____ of the circles are black.

5. _____ of the shapes are white.

Rewriting 2

ACTIVITY 18   Use the checklist below to check your paper. If the answer is "no" to any of these questions, change your paper. After you make the changes, give your paper to your teacher.

CHECKLIST

Content
Does your paper describe both the buildings and the people of your neighborhood?
Did you discuss the past and the future of your neighborhood?

Organization
Is your paper divided into paragraphs?
Do the paragraphs have clear topics?
Do the paragraphs have a topic sentence?

Grammar
Did you choose the correct verb tense for each verb?
Did you use the correct endings for each verb?
Did you form negative sentences correctly?
Did you use *many*, *some*, *more*, and *most* before nouns correctly?

Internet Activities

For additional activities related to this chapter, go to elt.thomson.com/catalyst.

A Sense of Place

ACTIVITY 1

Discussion Your "dream house" is the perfect house for you. In your dream, money is not a problem; you can have exactly the house you want. Working with a partner, describe your dream house to each other.

1. What does it look like?

2. What special features does it have?

Reading 1: Personal Experience Reading

Following is a letter from Miriam to her friend Jun Li.

Dear Jun Li,

1   I'm sorry I haven't written to you for so long! I have a lot of news to tell you about my life since we were students in the ESL Program together. My husband and I talked a long time about moving out of our old neighborhood, and finally we found an affordable house in a much safer neighborhood. Our old house was large and attractive. However, the area was getting more dangerous every day. We decided to leave, especially for our children's safety.

2   Our new house has a lot of things that I like. It has three bedrooms, one small bathroom, a living room and dining room, and a modern kitchen. Although it is smaller than the other house, it has some nice features. The small rooms are easy to keep clean, and we don't need to buy any new furniture for them. The new house is in good condition, so we did not need to repair much when we moved in. The heater and the roof are fine. There is a big yard in back of the house with some swings for our sons, and a small rock garden in front.

3   On the other hand, sometimes I feel annoyed by some things about the house. For example, the bathroom is so small that it's hard to turn around in there. The closets are so little that there is not enough room to put away the children's toys. The yard in the back has nice trees, but there is not enough space for the boys to run around. As a result, they play in the street instead. Worst of all, there are railroad tracks behind the house, so a train comes by every half-hour. The noise doesn't really bother me, but I don't like all those electric lines near the house.

4   Probably most important, the neighborhood feels safe and quiet. There are other children for my sons to play with, and most of the neighbors are helpful. However, they don't speak our language like the neighbors in our old neighborhood, and they have different customs from us. It's hard to find food from our country in this neighborhood. Sometimes I feel lonely here without people from my country to talk to.

5   Even though some things bother me about our new home, I'm glad we moved here because I feel much more secure. It's also easier to take care of this house.

6   I hope you can visit us here sometime soon because there is a new sofa bed for guests in the living room. I miss talking to you about our English classes together!

Love,
Miriam

Vocabulary

ACTIVITY 2 You may already know these words from Reading 1. To check your understanding, choose one of the words to fit in each sentence. After you are done, review your answers with your class.

affordable (adjective)	**yard** (noun)	**railroads** (noun)
attractive (adjective)	**swings** (noun)	**custom** (noun)
repair (verb)	**annoyed** (adjective)	**guests** (noun)
roof (noun)		

1. This city needs more _____ housing for poor people.

2. The teacher was _____ when the students didn't do their homework.

3. A dirty house for sale does not look _____ to buyers.

4. Calling people before you visit them is a _____ in the United States.

5. You should ask _____ in your home if they want something to eat or drink.

6. Many years ago travelers could take a train to most cities in the United

   States, but now there are not many _____.

7. I need to _____ the broken heater in my car.

8. There is a hole in the _____ of my house, so my bedroom gets wet when it rains.

9. Most children love to go up in the air on the _____ in the playground.

10. We keep our dog outside in the _____ when we leave the house.

ACTIVITY 3 **Academic Words** Read the sample sentences. They contain academic vocabulary that might be new to you. Then, in the sentences that follow, choose the academic word that fits best in the sentence. Review your answers with your class.

1. The people in that part of the city do not have much money. It is a poor **area**.

2. A **feature** is a special part of something. When we describe things, we often mention their **features**.

3. She studied at night for a long time. She was **finally** able to get her college degree.

4. When people feel **secure**, they feel safe from danger.

a. A young child cannot go to sleep unless he or she feels _____.

b. The U.S. Southwest is an _____ with a lot of Spanish influence.

c. She saved her money for many years. _____, she was able to get a new house.

d. One common _____ of a house in the suburbs is a big yard.

Discussion

ACTIVITY 3 Discuss these questions with a classmate. Your teacher may ask you to report on what you discussed.

1. What does Miriam like about her new home? What does she not like?

2. What do you like about your present home? What do you not like?

3. Do you think it is better for recent immigrants to live near people from their own country, so they feel comfortable? Or should they live among Americans to learn more about their language and customs?

Composition Analysis

Organization of a Letter A clear letter, like a good composition, has an organization that helps its reader. A letter begins with a greeting, usually "Dear _____." Many times, the first paragraph in a letter tells the reason for writing. Other paragraphs have topics, as in a composition. A letter ends with a closing, like a conclusion, which often gives good wishes to the person who will get the letter.

ACTIVITY 4 Answer these questions about the organization of Miriam's letter.

1. What is the topic of the first paragraph; that is, what is it mostly about?

   _____

2. What is the topic of the second paragraph?

   _____

3. The third paragraph?

   _____

4. The fourth paragraph?

_____

5. The fifth paragraph?

_____

Notice that **paragraph 6** is the friendly closing of Miriam's letter.

Writing 1

ACTIVITY 6

In the writing assignment in Activity 7, you will write a description of your home. To prepare for the assignment, write answers to the questions or instructions that follow. Make sure that your answers are in the form of sentences.

1. Do you live in a house or an apartment?

_____

_____

_____

2. Describe the biggest room in the place where you live.

_____

_____

_____

3. Describe the outside of your home.

_____

_____

_____

4. How do you feel about your neighborhood? Are you happy to live there?

_____

_____

_____

5. What do you like about your home?

_____

_____

_____

6. What do you not like about your home?

_____

_____

_____

7. Do you want to stay in your home, or do you want to move to a new home?

_____

_____

_____

ACTIVITY 7   **Writing Assignment** Write a letter to a friend about your present home. Choose a friend who has never seen the place where you live. You can use the outline below to help you write your letter.

1. Begin with a greeting (Dear _____) and an opening paragraph. In the opening paragraph, you can discuss how long it has been since you wrote, ask about your friend's family, or start the letter in some other way.

2. In the next 2–3 paragraphs, describe your home. You may want to write about the rooms and their size, the furniture in each room, etc.

3. In the next paragraph, tell about the outside of your home.

4. In the next paragraph, describe how you feel about your neighborhood.

5. In the next paragraph, describe what you like about your home and neighborhood.

6. In the next paragraph, describe what you don't like about your home and neighborhood.

7. In the next paragraph, tell your friend about your future: do you want to stay in your home, or do you want to move to a new home?

8. Finally, say goodbye to your friend in a closing paragraph. Make sure your letter has a closing expression at the end ("Love" or "Sincerely").

When you have finished, put your paper away for a while.

Grammar

There is and **there are**

We use the expressions *there is* and *there are* to show that something exists, and often, where it exists. For this reason you can often find prepositions (for example *on*, *in*, *under*) after *there is* or *there are*. For example, "There is a fly in my soup!" These expressions are very useful for descriptions of how things look. Here are some examples from Reading 1:

There is a big yard *in back of the house.*
There is not enough space *in the yard* for the boys to run around.
There are railroad tracks *behind the house.*
There are other children *in the neighborhood* for my sons to play with.
There is a new sofa bed *in the living room.*

Notice that we use *there is* when the noun that follows is singular (such as *yard*), and we use *there are* when the noun that follows is plural (such as *children*).

ACTIVITY 8   Write a description in several sentences of the people and things outside the window or door of the room where you are working now. Try to use *there is* or *there are* as part of your description. If the subject noun that comes after *there is* singular, use *is*. If the noun following *there* is plural, use *are*. Follow *there is* or *there are* with a prepositional phrase. The first two are done for you as examples.

1. *There are three students in the hallway.* _____

2. *There is a big tree outside on the street.* _____

3. _____

4. _____

5. _____

6. _____

7. _____

8. _____

The paragraphs below have some mistakes in the use of *there is* and *there are*. Find the mistakes and make corrections. (You should find four mistakes). Discuss your answers with your class.

My apartment is near the center of the city. Is a nice park near my building. There is a lot of young couples who live nearby, so there are a lot of children in the area.

Inside, my apartment is small. There is not many rooms. Is a living room, two bedrooms, and a kitchen.

Rewriting 1

ACTIVITY 10 Read your letter about your house again. Check your use of *there is* or *there are*. Be sure the verb *be* agrees with the subject noun after it, either singular or plural. If you do not have any sentences with *there is* or *there are*, put a few into your description.

Use the checklist below to review the changes you may need to make in your letter.

✓CHECKLIST

Content
Did you describe the inside of your home?
Did you describe the outside of your home?
Did you explain what you like and do not like about your home?

Organization
Is the paper divided into paragraphs?
Does each paragraph have a clear topic?

Grammar
Is each verb in the correct verb tense?
Does each verb have the correct ending?
Did you use *there is* and *there are* to tell where things are?

Reading 2: Academic Reading

This is an academic reading about the history of homes in the United States. It tells about the connections between the people who lived in different parts of the country and the kinds of homes they made.

Homes in the United States

1   When people come to the United States, they often have the idea that all homes here are new and beautiful. Sometimes they are shocked by the number of old houses in the United States, especially if they first arrive in a city. Both the new and old homes in the United States tell the story of the people who have settled here.

2   Although the United States is a young country compared to many other countries in the world, people have lived here for a very long time. Indians have lived in North America for at least 10,000 years. European settlers started to come here in the late 1500s. Over time, settlers came from many other countries to different parts of North America. They could not always find their usual building materials; therefore, they often had to change their style of building to fit their new environment.

3   Indians were the first people living in North America. They built different kinds of homes depending on the area where they lived. In the southwest part of what is now the United States, Pueblo Indians in the 1400s built houses on top of each other that looked almost like apartment buildings today. Their homes were built high on the sides of rocky cliffs so their enemies could not easily climb up to them. Their houses were made of dry

mud bricks which are called "adobe." The adobe bricks were warm in the winter and cool in the hot, dry summers of the Southwest. People in the Southwest still build houses in this "pueblo" style because it goes well with their environment.

4   The first European settlers, who were from Spain, came to what is now the state of Florida in the late 1500s. They tried to make the houses look like their houses in Spain, with light-colored walls, iron balconies[1], and heavy wooden

---

[1] A *balcony* is a place to sit that is on the outside of a building above the ground.

doors. Spanish settlers from Mexico settled in California in the 1700s. They built "missions," which were settlements started by religious leaders. These missions were also made in the Spanish style, with tile² floors and patios or gardens inside the walls of the house. However, the Spaniards had to change their material for building walls. Instead of stone, they used the local adobe. They stopped using straw³ and grass on their roofs when they saw that it was easy for Indians to set fire to the roofs when they were at war. Instead, they changed to red tile roofs.

5   English-speaking people were the largest group that settled the East Coast of North America in the seventeenth century. The first group who came lived in Virginia; later, another group came to Massachusetts. These early English settlers often made their first houses of long wood pieces or smaller wood pieces called "shingles." As their lives got better, they built brick houses that were more permanent. They usually copied the steep roofs, the design of the bricks, and the windows from the styles in England.

6   William Penn, a Quaker⁴ leader, was given land by the English king for a settlement in Pennsylvania which later became the city of Philadelphia. Penn recommended that settlers build brick houses with three rooms and corner fireplaces that could heat two rooms at one time. This type of townhouse was common in London in the late seventeenth century.

7   In the eighteenth and nineteenth centuries in the southern part of the United States (especially in Maryland, Virginia, and North and South Carolina), wealthy farmers, mostly from English backgrounds, owned "plantations." Plantations were big areas of land for farming tobacco, cotton, or food. Most work on the plantations was done by slaves from Africa. The owners lived in large homes, often made of brick. Most of the plantations had big porches in front and in back to catch any breezes in the hot weather of the South. In Louisiana, French plantation owners used a more French building style for

² A *tile* is a flat piece of clay.
³ *Straw* is a material made from dry grass.
⁴ The *Quaker* religion, the "Society of Friends," is a form of Christianity.

their homes. They built their wide porches, or balconies, on the second floor, which was the main living area, to get more air. Often there were fancy iron railings around these balconies.

8   Cities became much larger in the mid-nineteenth century because many more immigrants from Germany and western Europe were arriving to escape from wars or to find work. Many brick row houses were built for workers in the city factories. Middle-class people started to move out of the city's center into brownstone homes in neighborhoods with more space. A popular style of architecture (or building) was called "Victorian." Queen Victoria was the ruler of Britain for many years during that time. Victorian homes were usually made of brick or wood, with a lot of wooden decorations on the porches and roofs.

9   These Victorian-style houses belonged to middle or upper-class people; the poor people still lived in the center of cities, but their houses were old and often in bad condition. In Chicago and New York City, large, cheap apartment buildings were built as housing for the new immigrants from southern and central Europe. These apartment buildings did not have enough space for people to live in comfortably.

10   In the early twentieth century, more and more middle-class and poor people were moving to California. California had jobs, good weather, and more space for houses with back yards. However, there was a need for a new form of cheap single houses to go into these yards. The "bungalow" house style was the solution. Bungalows were one-story houses with low roofs and front porches. Because they were inexpensive and easy to build, bungalows were soon built in many other towns outside California.

11   By the middle of the twentieth century, American cities were getting old and crowded. People who had enough money moved to the suburbs outside the city. They could still travel into the city for work by car and train. The new houses in the suburbs often looked a lot like the old ranchers'[5] houses in the Southwest. They had one floor with no stairs. Like the "mission" style, they had an outdoor patio or a deck made of wood where the family could enjoy their back yard together. Large "housing developments" with many similar-looking ranch houses started to grow in the suburbs.

[5] A *rancher* owns a *ranch*, a large farm for cows and horses.

12 After a while, some people living in the suburbs got tired of having a house like all the other houses around them. They wanted to go back to the city where they could be closer to their workplaces. Also, city life seemed more exciting to young people than the quiet life of the suburbs. As a result, some suburban people bought old houses in the center of the city and fixed them up. The old neighborhoods downtown looked better, but the prices for rents went up. Poor people could not afford to live there anymore; they had to move to other parts of the city where houses were cheaper and in worse condition.

13 The homes from different times in the United States tell about the history of the country. Many of them remind us of the immigrants who built this country. American homes can tell their stories of the past and help us to understand the present.

Vocabulary

ACTIVITY 11   You probably already know most of the words in the list below. To check your understanding of these words, choose one of the words to complete the sentences. After you are done, review your answers with your class.

shocked (adjective)	**steep** (adjective)	**afford** (verb)
climb (verb)	**recommended** (verb)	**reminded** (verb)
brick (noun)	**slaves** (noun)	
permanent (adjective)	**solution** (noun)	

1. The road got higher very quickly. It was on a _____ hill.

2. The elevator was broken, so they had to _____ the stairs.

3. I almost forgot to go to class. My friend _____ me that it was time to go.

4. Moving to the suburbs was a _____ to the problems of living in the city.

5. The house was very nice, but they could not _____ to buy it.

6. The work on plantations was done by _____.

7. They planned to stay in their house for a long time. It was a _____ place to live.

8. She _____ that they look for a house in a safer neighborhood.

9. He was _____ when he found out the high price of the house.

10. _____ is a strong material for building houses.

Academic Words Read the sample sentences. They contain academic vocabulary that might be new to you. Then, in the sentences that follow, choose the academic word that fits best in each sentence. Review your answers with your class.

1. The **design** of the houses made them easy to protect.

2. The **environment** was cold and wet for five months a year.

3. The **style** of the farmers' homes was plain compared to the city houses.

4. His new job only lasted for a month; it was a **temporary** assignment.

a. The South was a good _____ for growing warm-weather plants.

b. Their clothes had an old-fashioned _____.

c. The cabin did not last for a long time. It was supposed to be a _____ home.

d. They thought of a _____ for the houses that allowed people to stay cool in the hot summer.

Discussion

ACTIVITY 13 These questions are about Reading 2. Discuss them with a partner. Your teacher may ask you to report on your answers.

1. Was any of the information in the reading surprising to you? Which groups of people and housing styles did you not know about before you read this article?

2. Which of the housing styles in the article have you seen before in the United States?

3. Which style of home in the article is most attractive to you?

Composition Analysis

Chronological Order Reading 2 contains information about different ethnic groups in North America and their homes. The paragraphs in the reading are organized according to national group and also according to time. There is information about the earlier groups earlier in the reading, and later groups are described later in the reading. To understand the reading well, you need to understand the order of each of the topics in the reading.

The chart below has a list of the people and places in North America that are described in Reading 2. Use the chart to make notes about when people settled an area and the features of the homes they made there. When you are finished, review the chart with your class.

People	Area of United States	Time	Features of Houses
Pueblo Indians	Southwest		
Spanish	Florida		
	California		
English	Virginia and Massachusetts		
	Pennsylvania		
	Maryland, Virginia, North and South Carolina		
French	Louisiana		
People from the eastern United States	California		
People from the U.S. cities	Suburbs		
People from the suburbs	Cities		

Writing 2

ACTIVITY 15

In the writing assignment in Activity 16, you will describe the outside of a house. You will choose a house that is in your neighborhood (not your own home), and describe it. To help you prepare for this assignment, answer the questions that follow. Write complete sentences when you answer the questions.

1. Is the home a single house, a duplex (a twin or double house), or is it a row house (connected to a lot of other houses)?

   _____

2. How many floors does it have?

   _____

3. Are there a lot of windows?

   _____

4. What features from the chart in Activity 14 do you see in the building? For instance, does it have a steep roof, a big porch, etc.?

   _____

   _____

   _____

5. What century do you think it was built in?

   _____

6. What do you think about the history of this house? Was it made for a wealthy, middle-class, or poor family?

   _____

ACTIVITY 16

Writing Assignment Write a composition of several paragraphs that describes the same house you wrote about in Activity 15. Be sure to:

Describe how the house looks from the outside, including the style, the materials it was built from, the number of floors, etc.

Describe the features in Reading 2 that you can see in the house. (You can see a list of features in your answers to Activity 14.) What can you understand about the history of the house from these features?

When you are finished with your composition, put it aside for a while.

Grammar

Contrast Expressions

Expressions such as *but*, *although*, and *even though* connect two different ideas that contrast. They are used to combine short sentences into a longer sentence. Here are examples:

> The yard in the back has nice trees, **but** there is not enough space for the boys to run around.
>
> The old neighborhoods downtown looked better, **but** the prices for rents went up.
>
> I did not do very well on the test **although** I studied hard.

Although and *even though* mean the same thing and are used the same way:

> I did not do very well on the test **even though** I studied hard.

Notice that the part of the sentence that begins with *although* can come at the beginning of the sentence:

> **Although** the United States is a young country compared to many other countries in the world, people have lived here for a very long time.

ACTIVITY 17 Use a contrast expression to combine, or put together, the following pairs of sentences into one sentence. Think of two different ways to combine each pair of sentences and write them both. (The first one is done as an example.) Use these contrast expressions:

although	**but**	**even though**

1. Some people could buy a house.

   Many people did not earn enough money.

   Although some people could buy a house, many people did not earn enough money.

   Some people could buy a house, but many people did not earn enough money.

2. Workers still lived in smaller houses in the city.

   Middle-class people moved outside the city.

   _____

   _____

   _____

   _____

3. California had more space for houses with back yards.

   In the East Coast cities, people still lived in high-rise apartment buildings.

   _____

   _____

   _____

   _____

4. People often expect houses in the United States to be beautiful.

   There are many old houses in the cities that need repairs.

   _____

   _____

   _____

   _____

5. The United States is younger than many countries in the world.

   Europeans have been living in North America for about 400 years.

   _____

   _____

   _____

   _____

6. Houses in the eastern cities usually have several floors.

   Many houses in the West have only one floor.

   _____

   _____

   _____

   _____

Rewriting 2

ACTIVITY 18 Read the composition you wrote about the house in Activity 16. Use the checklist below to review the changes you need to make in your paper.

CHECKLIST

Content

Did you describe the outside of the house?

Did you connect this house to one of the housing styles you read about in this chapter?

Did you write what you think about the history of this house?

Organization

Is the paper divided into paragraphs?

Does each paragraph have a clear topic?

Grammar

Is each verb in the correct verb tense?

Does each verb have the correct ending?

Are *there is* and *there are* used correctly to tell where things are on the outside of the house?

Did you use contrast expressions correctly?

Internet Activities

For additional activities related to this chapter, go to elt.thomson.com/catalyst.

CHAPTER

6 Living Without Fear

Exploring the Topic

ACTIVITY 1

Discussion The first reading in this chapter is about something frightening that happened in a city neighborhood. Before you read it, discuss these questions with your class.

1. Do you feel safe where you live? Why or why not?

2. What are the reasons why people commit crimes?

3. Tell the story of a real crime. What was the cause of this crime?

Reading 1: Personal Experience Reading

What Really Happened?

1   Last night there was a shooting in a grocery store. The store is owned by an Asian man. The store owner, Minh Le, shot a man who lives in the neighborhood. The neighborhood man, Paul Williams, was hurt, but he did not die. Many people in the neighborhood are upset about the shooting.

2   Mr. Le's daughter was at the store when the shooting happened. She called an ambulance and the police after the shooting. When the police arrived at the store, they talked to Mr. Le and two witnesses who saw what happened. They asked all three people to tell what they saw. A police officer wrote down what they said. The three witnesses said different things, but they tried to tell the truth. This is what each person told the police officer.

The Store Owner's Story

3   At about 11:00 at night, a man and a woman came into my store. I think the man was drunk. He talked very loudly and his behavior was strange. I felt scared because I did not know what was wrong with him.

4   The man came up to the counter and asked for a pack of cigarettes. I handed the cigarettes to him, and I told him the price. Then he reached into his pocket and said, "Empty the cash register." He started to take his gun out of his

pocket. I shouted at him, and I pulled my gun from under the counter. I was very frightened. I shot him. Then my daughter called the police.

5   There are a lot of bad people in this neighborhood. We have drunks and we have drug addicts. I was robbed six times this year. I am lucky I did not get shot. I couldn't stand there and let this man shoot me.

A Neighborhood Woman's Story

6   Tonight I went with my neighbor, Paul, to his daughter's graduation. We went to a party after the graduation to celebrate.

7   On the way home, we stopped at the grocery store so that Paul could get some cigarettes. Paul went up to the counter and asked for a pack of cigarettes. The man said, "Four fifty." Paul said, "Four fifty! What do you mean 'Four fifty'! Cigarettes cost four dollars at most! I have a pack right here in my pocket that I bought for three fifty." He started to take the cigarettes out of his pocket. Then Paul said, "I'm so tired of you people. You people come into our neighborhood, take our money, and you get rich. You don't even live here." He started talking like that. He always gets upset when people try to cheat him.

8   After Paul spoke to the man about the price, the man got very angry. The man yelled, but I didn't understand what he said. He took something from under the counter. Then he shot Paul.

9   I don't understand why this happened. That night Paul was so happy about his daughter, he was in a really good mood. I can't believe someone shot him. He wasn't doing anything wrong, and now he's in the hospital.

Mr. Le's Daughter's Story

10   Earlier tonight a man and a woman came into the store. I didn't know them. The man asked for some cigarettes, and my father told him the price. The man started to complain about the price. He was yelling at my father, and I got scared.

11   I started to walk to the counter. My father yelled at the man. I saw the man take something from his pocket. I thought he was going to shoot my father. My father got his gun and shot the man first.

12   I was so scared. We get robbed a lot in this store. I am sorry the man was hurt, but he was wrong to threaten my father.

Vocabulary

ACTIVITY 2 You probably already know the words below. To check your understanding of these words, choose one of the words to fit in each sentence. After you are done, review your answers with your class.

pack (noun)   **angry** (adjective)

shouts (verb)   **complaining** (verb)

cheat (verb)

1. He was unhappy, and he was talking loud. He seemed _____.

2. They are talking about a problem. They are explaining why they are

   unhappy. They are _____.

3. He was not fair. He did not want to work hard. He tried to _____.

4. He always talks very loud. He _____.

5. They sell six pieces of chewing gum together. The gum comes in

   a _____.

ACTIVITY 3 **Academic Words** Read the sample sentences. They contain academic vocabulary in **boldface** that might be new to you. Then, in the sentences that follow, choose the word from the list that fits best in each sentence. Review your answers with your class.

1. A **witness** is a person who sees or hears something that happens, and then tells about it later. Often **witnesses** speak in court about what they saw or know.

2. People's **behavior** is the things that they do. **Behavior** is a kind of action that we can see, hear, or feel with our senses.

3. My brother's fast driving **frightens** me. I don't like to drive with him in his car.

4. When someone **threatens** us, we feel that they may do something bad to us. Sometimes people **threaten** others on purpose to get what they want.

a. She was there when the accident happened. She was a _____.

b. He says he will hurt me if I do not do what he wants. He is trying

   to _____ me.

c. I am afraid of him. I don't feel safe when he is around. He _____ me.

d. His _____ made me think he was sick. He was coughing, and he asked to sit down.

Discussion

ACTIVITY 4   Discuss these questions about Reading 1 as a class.

1. Which of the stories do you believe the most? What really happened the night Mr. Williams was shot?

2. Did Paul Williams do anything wrong? If yes, what did he do wrong? Did the store owner, Minh Le, do anything wrong? If yes, what did he do wrong?

3. Why was Paul Williams shot? How could people in this neighborhood stop bad events like this from happening?

Composition Analysis

Narration: Topics, Paragraphs, and Topic Sentences   The story about the shooting in the store tells about events. As you saw in Chapter 4, a story that describes events is called a **narration**. A narration is divided into paragraphs, like other kinds of writing. The topics of the paragraphs are the parts of the story that happened at about the same time. There can be more than one way to divide a narration into paragraphs. The writer must decide which events fit together.

It is not always easy to see the topic in a narrative paragraph. Many times the writer will tell what happened without a clear topic sentence.

These are the topics of the paragraphs in the report made to the police by the store owner.

Paragraph	Topic
3	What happened when the man came in the store
4	What happened when the owner shot the man
5	The owner's reason for shooting the man

ACTIVITY 5   Write down the topics of the paragraphs in the other reports.

The Neighborhood Woman's Story

Paragraph	Topic
6	_____
7	_____
8	_____
9	_____

Minh Le's Daughter's Story
Paragraph   Topic

10 _____

11 _____

12 _____

Review your answers with a classmate, and then with your teacher.

Writing 1

ACTIVITY 6   In the writing assignment for this section, you will write about the story in Reading 1. Before you start to write, you need to decide what you think really happened at the store that night. Write sentences to answer these questions.

1. Why did Mr. Williams come into the store?

   _____

2. Did Mr. Williams shout at Mr. Le?

   _____

3. Did Mr. Williams try to rob the store?

   _____

4. Did Mr. Williams have a gun?

   _____

ACTIVITY 7   **Writing Assignment** Write a composition about the shooting in the grocery store. There are three topics to write about in your paper:

- What happened? (Use the information from the three reports. When you write, you must decide for yourself what you think really happened.)

- Who is wrong in this situation, Mr. Le or Mr. Williams?

- What punishment will you give the person who is wrong?

These are some steps you can follow in planning your paper.

First, write some notes about each one of these topics. When you write about what happened, write down each event in the story. For example, you might write:

Paul Williams went to his daughter's graduation

He went to the store to get cigarettes

He got angry about the price of the cigarettes

When you write about who was wrong in this situation, you might write:

Mr. Williams was wrong. He was angry and Mr. Le was afraid.

or:

Mr. Le was wrong. Mr. Williams did not have a gun or weapon.

After you write your notes, use them to write a composition. Each paragraph in your composition should have a different topic. When you are finished with your story, put it aside. You will make some changes later.

Grammar

Simple Past Tense with Negative

Look at these sentences, and notice that they contain the word *not*:

Mr. Williams **did not die**.
Mr. Le **did not understand** him.
The cigarettes **did not cost** too much.
His friend **did not come** in the store.
Mr. Williams **did not have** a gun.

These sentences are in the simple past tense. Each sentence is also *negative*, which means that it includes *not*.

For most verbs, negative sentences in the simple past tense include *did*. The form of *did* is the same if the subject of the sentence is singular or plural. Also, notice that the form of the main verb (*die, understand, cost,* etc.) is the *simple* or *base form*. There are no endings on the main verb.

ACTIVITY 8

Write answers to these questions about the story. If your answer is "no," write past tense negative sentences. If the answer is "yes," write past tense sentences without *not*. Do not put "yes" or "no" at the beginning of your answer to each question. The first one is done for you.

1. Did Mr. Williams die?

   Mr. Williams did not die.

2. Did Mr. Williams try to rob the store?

   _____

3. Did Mr. Williams shout at Mr. Le?

   _____

4. Did Mr. Le think Mr. Williams was happy?

   _____

5. Did Mr. Williams ask for cigarettes?

_____

6. Did Mr. Le shoot Mr. Williams?

_____

7. Did Mr. Williams say, "Empty the cash register"?

_____

8. Did Mr. Williams have a gun?

_____

9. Did Mr. Williams threaten Mr. Le?

_____

Compare your answers with your classmates. You might agree or disagree with their answers. Keep your answers to the questions. You will use them later when you rewrite your composition.

ACTIVITY 9   Read the following paragraph. There are mistakes in three past tense negative verb forms. Correct the mistakes in the composition. Review your answers with your class.

Last night there was an accident in town. Mr. Le owns a store in the city. He shot a customer, Mr. Williams, while Mr. Williams was in his store. Mr. Le not want to hurt anyone. Mr. Le thought that Mr. Williams was a robber. Mr. Williams was angry about the price of cigarettes, but he did not wanted to rob Mr. Le. When Mr. Williams shouted, Mr. Le got scared. He shot Mr. Williams. Luckily, Mr. Williams not died.

Rewriting 1

Now you will do some more work on the writing assignment from Activity 7.

Organization Read your story again. Review Activity 5 in "Composition Analysis" above. Is your story divided into paragraphs? Does each paragraph tell a different part of the story, or talk about a different topic? If not, you will need to change your paper. Rewrite it so that each paragraph has a clear topic. You may want to add some new details to your story when you rewrite.

Grammar Many of the verbs in your story should be in the past tense. Past tense verbs will be in all the parts where you described what happened on the night of the shooting. Underline each verb in your story. Decide if each verb should be in the past tense or the present tense. Then make sure that you form each verb correctly. Did you use the correct form of regular or irregular verbs? If you are not sure, you can use Appendix 2, a good dictionary, or a grammar book, or you can ask your teacher. Also, review Activities 8 and 9 on past tense verbs. You can use them to check for past tense sentences with negative.

Use the checklist below to answer questions about your paper. If the answer is "no" to any of the questions, make changes in your paper. When you are finished, give your paper to your teacher.

✓CHECKLIST

Content

Did you describe what you think happened at the store the night of the shooting?

Did you explain who you think was wrong in this situation?

Did you explain what you think is the right punishment for the person who was wrong?

Organization

Is your paper divided into paragraphs?

Do the paragraphs have clear topics?

Grammar

Did you choose the correct verb tense for each verb?

Did you use the correct endings for each verb, including past tense?

Did you use negative verb forms correctly?

When you are ready, hand in your paper to your teacher.

Reading 2: Academic Reading

The following is an academic reading that discusses the causes of crime. Preview the reading. Here are some things to think about as you preview.

1. What is the topic of the reading? How do you know?

2. Look at the different sections, or parts, of the reading. How many ideas about the causes of crime does the reading discuss?

3. Look at the graph in the reading. What does the graph show?

After you finish previewing, read the story carefully.

Causes of Crime

1   Sociology is the study of people in groups. It is the study of families, communities, and national groups. People who study sociology are called sociologists. One of the topics that sociologists study is the causes of crime.

2   Crime is a serious problem in the United States. The United States has more crime than other countries. For example, Americans commit murder more often than people who live in Europe or Japan. Also, there are many more robberies in the United States than in Germany or Great Britain. There are fewer robberies in Denmark, Switzerland, and the Netherlands than in the United States.

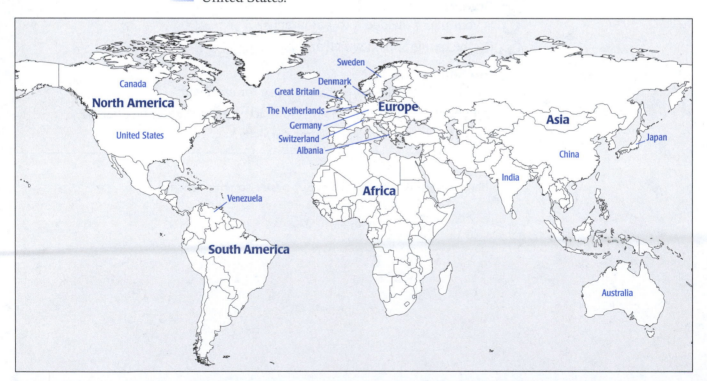

3   Usually rich countries have less crime, and poor countries have more crime. The United States is rich, but it has the same amount of crime as very poor countries. Sociologists wonder why there is so much crime in the United States. They don't agree on the answer. Following are some of the answers that sociologists and other people give to explain the causes of crime.

American customs and history are full of violence.

4   Some people believe that violence is natural for Americans. Our country began with violence. The first Americans fought Indians for the land, and they fought British soldiers for their independence. Americans even fought against each other in the Civil War. Perhaps we have so much crime because violence is part of our history.

5   Many sociologists say that this idea is wrong. Other countries also have violence in their history, and they do not have the problems that we have. For example, Australia also has violence in its past, but it has little violence today. Canada has a history that is similar to the United States, but it has very few murders.

There are too many guns in the United States.

6   Some people say that we have so much violence because we have too many guns. Guns are a part of our culture. Many American people believe they have a right to have their own gun. They want to protect themselves, or they want to have guns for hunting or sports. It is easy for honest people to buy guns, but it is also easy for criminals to get guns. Criminals often use guns when they rob people or commit other crimes.

7   Other people say that guns are not the real problem. These people say that criminals can use any kind of weapon, not just guns, to commit crimes. For example, more people in California are killed by knives than by guns.

Poverty and inequality cause crime.

8   Some sociologists say that poverty causes crime. When many people lose their jobs, crime increases. They say the real cause of crime is poverty.

9   Also, some sociologists say that inequality causes crime. When people are unequal, crime increases. The United States is rich, but we have more inequality than other rich countries. There is a big difference between the lives of poor people and other people in the United States.

We have more crime because we do not punish criminals.

10   Some people say that we do not punish people who commit crimes enough. They say that our system is too kind to criminals. Many criminals do not go to prison because there is no room left in prison.

11   It is true that most people who commit crimes do not go to jail. In the United States there are about thirty-five million crimes every year. People only report about fifteen million of these crimes to the police. Police arrest three million people for serious crimes, and two million are punished. Only 500,000 go to prison. This means that less than two percent of criminals go to prison.

12 Other people say that strong punishment does not make less crime. The United States has a lot of crime, but we put more people in jail than any other country. We put more and more people in jail every year. Sociologists count the number of people in jail in each country. They usually count the number of people in jail for every 100,000 people who live in a country. The chart below shows the number of people in jail in several countries.

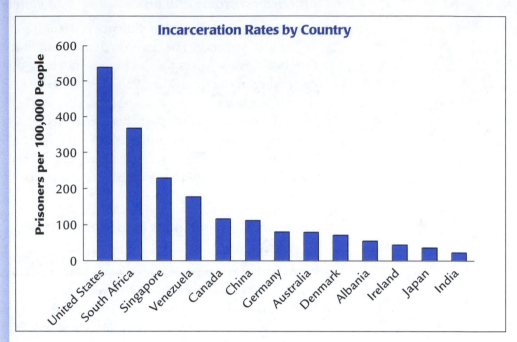

We have more crime because we do not punish our children.

13 Some people say that the United States has a lot of crime because we do not teach our children what is right and wrong. They say that parents are afraid to punish their children. If people hit their children, the children will call the police.

14 But other people say this is wrong. In the United States, parents punish their children more than parents in other rich countries. For example, parents in Sweden or Denmark do not hit their children often. These countries have very little crime.

We have more crime because our prisons are schools for criminals.

15 Some people say that our prisons do not help with our crime problem. They say that prisons make crime worse. When people go to jail they do not learn to stay away from crime. They learn to be better criminals. When they leave prison, they are angry and unhappy. Many criminals use drugs. They do not stop using drugs in prison because there are not enough doctors to help them stop.

16 Other people do not agree with this. They say that prison is a good punishment because it teaches people to respect the law. They say that we should have more prisons, and keep criminals in prison longer.

Solutions

17   Some sociologists think that there are solutions for the crime problem. They say that people do not commit crimes when they feel part of a community. When families and neighborhoods are strong, crime is low.

18   Some sociologists say that we can fight crime if we fight inequality. If the government or other groups helped people to be more equal, there would be less crime.

Vocabulary

ACTIVITY 11   You probably already know the words below. To check your understanding of these words, choose one of the words to fit in the sentences. After you are done, review your answers with your class.

crime (noun)	**honest** (adjective)	**worse** (adjective)
murder (here, a noun)	**weapon** (noun)	**solution** (noun)
customs (noun)	**knife** (noun)	**government** (noun)
violence (noun)	**prison** (noun)	
hunting (noun)	**arrest** (here, a verb)	

1. A _____ is a tool that people use for cutting.

2. The police _____ drivers who go ninety miles an hour.

3. The law says that people cannot steal. Stealing is a _____.

4. The _____ makes the laws, and also makes sure that people follow them.

5. The act of killing another person is _____.

6. A thing that people use to fight or kill is a _____.

7. When a person commits a crime, he or she may be put in _____.

8. Murder is a _____ crime than robbery.

9. A person who tells the truth and does not steal is _____.

10. The rules that people follow when they belong to a group or a culture

    are _____.

11. _____ is the act of killing wild animals.

12. _____ is an action that causes harm or injury to another person.

13. A way to improve something or to help with a problem is a _____.

Academic Words Read the sample sentences. They contain academic vocabulary in **boldface** that might be new to you. Then, in the sentences that follow, choose the word from the list that fits best in the sentence. Review your answers with your class.

1. When people **commit** a crime, they act in a way that is against the law.

2. A **civil** war is a war between groups inside one nation.

3. We **punish** someone when we do something negative to them to change their behavior, or to teach them about right and wrong.

4. A **community** is a group of people who are connected to each other. People in a community work together, spend time together, and are similar to each other in some way.

a. When a _____ works together to stop crime, people feel safer.

b. One reason for _____ war in a country is fighting among different religious groups.

c. When people kill, and they know they are doing something wrong, they

_____ the crime of murder.

d. Some parents send their children to their rooms to be quiet when they want

to _____ them for bad behavior.

Discussion

Discuss these questions with your class.

1. What is a crime? Agree on a definition as a class.

2. What are examples of crimes that affect you personally?

3. Is there more crime in the United States than in other countries?

4. What causes people to commit crimes?

Composition Analysis

Point of View This reading is like a discussion between two people who have different points of view. For example, some paragraphs explain an idea about a cause of crime. Other paragraphs explain why the idea could be wrong. When students read this discussion, they should understand both points of view, the reasons "for and against" each idea. Academic writing often has information that explains how people disagree with each other.

ACTIVITY 14   Look at the reading again. Try to find the main idea of paragraphs 4 through 16. Some examples are given for paragraphs 4–6.

Paragraph 4   *We have crime because our history is violent.*

Paragraph 5   *Other countries have a violent history, but they do not have much crime.*

Paragraph 6   *We have crime because we have too many guns.*

Paragraph 7   _____

Paragraph 8   _____

Paragraph 9   _____

Paragraph 10 _____

Paragraph 11 _____

Paragraph 12 _____

Paragraph 13 _____

Paragraph 14 _____

Paragraph 15 _____

Paragraph 16 _____

When you are finished, review your list with your class.

Writing 2

In the writing assignment for this section, you will write about your opinions relating to crime. To practice writing sentences that show your opinion, write sentences to answer the questions that follow. You can use these verbs to say your opinion about an idea: *agree, think, believe*. For example:

I agree that American customs are a cause of crime.

I do not agree that the number of guns is a cause of crime.

1. Is violence "natural" for Americans?

   _____

2. Are there too many guns in the United States?

   _____

3. Does poverty cause crime?

   _____

4. Does inequality cause crime?

   _____

5. Does the United States punish people who commit crimes enough?

   _____

6. Do people in the United States punish their children enough?

   _____

7. Do prisons stop people from committing crimes?

   _____

Writing Assignment Write a composition about the causes of crime in the United States. Explain the reasons for your opinions about crime.

In your paper, you should discuss some of the causes of crime that you read about in Reading 2. Do you think these things are the causes of crime? At the end of your paper, write about things that can solve the problem of crime. When you are finished, set your paper aside for a while.

Grammar

Cause and Effect Expressions

Reading 2 gives some ideas about the causes of crime. Below are some sentences from the reading.

> We have so much crime **because** violence is part of our history.
> We have so much violence **because** we have too many guns.
> We have more crime **because** we do not punish criminals.

In these sentences, the writer joins two short sentences into a longer sentence. Each of the two parts of the new sentence is called a *clause*. The writer connects the two parts with the word *because* to show that the second part, or clause, is the reason for the first clause.

We have so much violence	**because**	we have too many guns.
clause	**because**	*clause*

Notice that the sentence begins with a capital letter and ends with a period. Notice that there are no commas or other marks before or after *because*.

Other sentences use the word *cause* to show the same connection. Sometimes *cause* can be a verb. For example:

> Poverty **causes** crime.
> Inequality **causes** crime.

Sometimes *cause* can be used as a noun. It is used with *of*:

> The real **cause of** crime is poverty.

ACTIVITY 17 Practice using *cause and effect* expressions. Work with a partner and discuss the statements in the chart below. First decide if you think each statement is true. Then write a sentence in the chart about the second question, "Does this cause crime in the United States?" Use the connector *because* or the verb *cause*. When you are finished, discuss your answers with your class.

	Is this true?	Does this cause crime in the United States?
1. American customs and history are full of violence.	Yes	*America's history does not cause crime.*
2. There are too many guns in the United States.		
3. There is poverty and inequality here.		
4. We do not punish criminals enough.		
5. We do not punish our children when they do wrong.		
6. Our prisons are schools for criminals.		

Rewriting 2

ACTIVITY 18 Review your answers to Activity 17. Compare these sentences to the composition you wrote in Activity 16. You may want to add some of these sentences to your composition.

Use the checklist below to answer questions about your paper. You and your partner can use this checklist to comment on each other's papers, too. If the answer is "no" to any of the questions, make changes in your paper. When you are finished, give your paper to your teacher.

CHECKLIST

Content
Did you discuss the reasons for crime in the United States?
Did you discuss some things that are *not* causes of crime?

Organization
Is your paper divided into paragraphs?
Do the paragraphs have clear topics?
Does each paragraph have a topic sentence?

Grammar
Did you choose the correct verb tense for each verb?
Did you use the correct endings for each verb?
Did you use cause and effect expressions correctly?

Internet Activities

For additional activities related to this chapter, go to elt.thomson.com/catalyst.

7 Paved with Gold?

Exploring the Topic

ACTIVITY 1

Discussion This chapter is about life in the United States. Discuss these questions with your class.

1. Is the United States a good place to work and make money?

2. Is it a good country to find a place to live?

3. Are people in the United States safe?

Reading 1: Personal Experience Reading

This reading is about a man's thoughts and feelings about his new life in the United States.

A Story of Two Letters

1   Pierre came to the United States from Haiti. He lives with his younger brother, Gary. When he came here, Pierre was surprised. America was big, and fast. Some things were better than his image of America before he arrived there, but some things were not as good.

2   Some things in Pierre's new life were very good. Pierre felt free to do and say what he wanted to. He was able to earn enough money to buy a car. He bought a house in an old neighborhood. His life was still hard, but it was more peaceful than his life in Haiti.

3   On the other hand, the country was not as rich as Pierre expected. He was surprised that the cities were sometimes dirty and dangerous. He and his brother had trouble with money. Pierre felt that he spent most of his time at work.

4   One day Pierre got a letter from his youngest brother, Jean. Jean wanted to ask Pierre an important question: he wanted to know if he should come to America. Pierre wrote back:

Dear Jean:

5   I received your letter today. I am glad you are well, and that you are taking good care of our parents.

6   You want to know if you should come to America. The answer is "yes." I have enough money for you to join us here in our new house. You should come.

7   I will tell you the most important reason to come. Here you will be able to make your own decisions. People here do not need to ask permission before they do something new. If you feel something is right, you can do it. You can take a risk. Also, there is no pressure to follow traditions if you don't want to. If a tradition seems good to you, you can follow it. If not, you can forget it.

8   There is another reason to come here. People do not live with fear. You can walk the streets any time of the day or night, and no one will bother you. You don't have to lock your door. You don't have to be afraid.

9   I can give you one other reason. This country is full of good places to live. My house is small, and it is old, but it is much better than our house at home, and it belongs to me!

10   I have done very well here, and I know you will also do well. I have a job. I have my own house. America is a clean, rich, happy place if you are ready to work hard.

Love,
Your Brother

---

11   When Pierre finished his letter, he put it away and went to sleep.

12   The next day, Pierre came home late from work. It was almost dark when he got to his street. He saw young men standing on the corner. He didn't like the way they looked. He ate a meal of cold pizza, but he wished he could have some delicious chicken and rice from Haiti. He looked at the day's mail. There were no letters, only bills. He spoke to his younger brother, and they got in an argument.

13   After a while he went upstairs to his room. He saw his letter to Jean on his desk, and he read it again. He felt bad about the letter and about his life. He decided to write a new letter:

Dear Jean:

14   I received your letter today. I am glad you are well, and that you are taking good care of our parents.

15   You want to know if you should come to America. The answer is "no." I think you should stay home and go to school. There is nothing for you here.

16   I will tell you the most important reason to stay home. Here you will be alone, even if you live with other people. You will be "free" to solve your own problems. This means no one will help you when you are in trouble. No one here cares about their friends or family. Everyone has their own problems.

17   There is another reason to stay in Haiti. People in America live with fear. Every day I have to look over my shoulder when I walk on the street. People steal from each other. Everyone locks their door when they come home. They are afraid to leave the house at night. America is a big jail.

18   I sometimes think it was a mistake for me to come here. I have a job, but I feel that my work helps only others, not me. I have my own house, but I don't even know my neighbors. They say that the streets in America are paved with gold. I have not seen any gold yet. America is hard. Stay home.

Love,
Your Brother

---

19   Pierre looked at the letter. He picked up yesterday's letter, and he read it again. He held the two letters in his hands. Which one is the truth? Which one will he send?

Vocabulary

ACTIVITY 2 You probably already know the words below. To check your understanding of these words, choose one of the words to fit in each sentence. After you are done, review your answers with your class.

earn (verb)   **meal** (noun)
lock (here, a verb) **argument** (noun)
corner (noun)   **mistake** (noun)

1. Her pay was low. She did not _____ enough money to pay her rent.

2. Our neighborhood is safe. People do not _____ their doors at night.

3. I said today is Tuesday, although it is really Monday. I made a _____.

4. They got very angry while they were talking. They had an _____.

5. Some people say that breakfast in the most important _____ because it gives a good beginning to the day.

6. Their house is at the _____ of two big streets.

ACTIVITY 3 **Academic Words** Read the sample sentences. They contain academic vocabulary in **boldface** that might be new to you. Then choose the academic word or phrase that fits best in the sentences that follow. Review your answers with your class.

1. When people have an **image** of something, they have a picture in their mind.

2. A customer **asked permission** to smoke in the restaurant.

3. A **risk** is a situation or an action in which something negative can happen.

a. When he got to California, he was surprised how different it seemed from his _____ of the state.

b. They were not sure the new idea would work. They decided to take a _____.

c. He _____ to leave work a little early.

Discussion

ACTIVITY 4 Discuss these questions with your class.

1. What are the good things Pierre sees in the United States? Do you agree with him?

2. What are the bad things Pierre sees in the United States? Do you agree with him about these problems?

3. On two different days, Pierre has different feelings about his life in the United States. Can you understand why he has different feelings? Do you sometimes change your ideas about your life here?

4. Which letter should Pierre send? Or should he write a new letter that is different from the first two?

Composition Analysis

Contrasting Different Ideas About the Same Topic In Reading 1, Pierre writes two letters. Even though the ideas in the two letters are different, the topics are the same. For example, paragraph 6 and paragraph 15 have the same topic: both paragraphs are about whether Jean should come to the United States. However, the main ideas of the two paragraphs are different. The main idea of paragraph 6 is that Jean should come to the United States. The main idea of paragraph 15 is that Jean should stay home. When you analyze a piece of writing, it is important to see the difference between the **topic** and the **main idea**.

ACTIVITY 5 The story in this chapter has several parts. There are two letters and three narrative sections in the story. Each paragraph has a topic. Write the topic of the paragraphs listed below.

Paragraph 2 _____

Paragraph 3 _____

Paragraph 7 _____

Paragraph 8 _____

Paragraph 16 _____

Paragraph 17 _____

Discuss your answers with your class.

ACTIVITY 6 Work with a partner. Write notes on Pierre's different ideas about living in the United States in his two letters.

Pierre's experiences and ideas about freedom in the United States

First letter:

_____

_____

Second letter:

_____

_____

Pierre's experiences and ideas about finding a good, safe place to live in the United States

First letter:

_____

_____

Second letter:

_____

_____

Pierre's experiences and ideas about earning money in the United States

First letter:

_____

_____

Second letter:

_____

_____

Writing Assignment Write a composition discussing Pierre's different feelings about life in the United States. Explain whether you agree or disagree with what he says.

You can use the topics of his two letters as paragraph topics in your composition. One way to organize the composition is explained below.

Introductory Paragraph (the important idea of the whole composition)

Pierre has different feelings and ideas about his life in the United States depending on the experiences he has on a good or bad day. I also have some feelings and ideas about my own experiences of life in this country.

Paragraph 1

Are your feelings about freedom in the United States more positive, like Pierre's first letter, or more negative, like his second letter? Explain why.

Paragraph 2

Are your experiences in finding a good, safe place to live in the United States more positive, like Pierre's first letter, or more negative, like his second letter? Explain why.

Paragraph 3

Are your experiences about jobs and earning money in the United States more positive, like Pierre's first letter, or more negative, like his second letter? Explain why.

Concluding Paragraph

In general, are your feelings about your life in the United States more positive or negative?

Grammar

Comparison with Adjectives

In Pierre's story, there are many **comparisons**. Pierre writes about the difference between things. When he says his life in America is "more peaceful than Haiti," he is comparing two lives. Look at the comparisons in these phrases and sentences from the reading:

1 It was **more peaceful than** Haiti.
2 ... from his **younger** brother
3 It is **better than** our house.
4 Some things were **not as good**.
5 It was **not as rich as he expected**.

Most English adjectives can be used in a comparison. For most longer adjectives, we make a comparison by adding the word *more* before the adjective. We use the word *than* when we include both parts of a comparison in one phrase or sentence. For example:

more peaceful: His life was **more peaceful than** his sister's.
more dangerous: America is **more dangerous than** Europe.
more secure: This neighborhood is **more secure than** my old one.
more interesting: This book is **more interesting than** the history book.
more helpful: Her teacher is **more helpful than** my teacher.

Some adjectives add the ending *-er* to make a comparison. Generally, short words use *-er* in comparisons, and longer words use *more*. You may need to use a dictionary to find out which form is correct.

younger   older   richer   bigger   nicer

There are a few adjectives that use a different form for comparisons. For example, the comparative form of *good* is *better*. The comparative form of *bad* is *worse*.

Notice that in Pierre's story, comparatives sometimes are used with *not*. For example, if we describe the squares below, we could say:

B is **bigger** than A.

However, we could also say:

A is **not as big as** B.

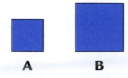

Note how negative comparisons use *as* before and after the regular form of the adjective.

ACTIVITY 8

Write sentences that use comparisons. Think about people that you know. Write four sentences that compare these people to each other. Use *not as* in some of your sentences. You can use the examples from the grammar section to help you. One example sentence is done for you.

1. *My brother is not as tall as my father.*

2. _____

_____

3. _____

_____

4. _____

_____

5. _____

_____

ACTIVITY 9

The paragraphs below have some mistakes in the forms of the comparative adjectives. Find the mistakes and make corrections. (You should find four mistakes.) Discuss your answers with your class.

I am happy about the place where I live right now. My house is more good than where I used to live. First of all, my new house is more big than my new house. It is more newer and it is in a nicer neighborhood. Also, the rooms are bigger and in better condition.

On the other hand, there were some things about the old house that I liked better. The neighborhood was not as safer, but it was more active. My life at home is comfortable now, but it is not as interesting.

Rewriting 1

ACTIVITY 10 Look at the composition you wrote about life in the United States. Check to make sure that each paragraph has its own topic.

Look for places where you used comparisons. Make sure you formed those sentences correctly.

You can use the checklist below to help you remember the important things you want to include in your paper. If the answer to any of these questions is "no," make changes in your paper.

CHECKLIST

Content

Did you write your opinion about earning money in the United States?

Did you write your opinion about places to live in the United States?

Did you write your opinion about freedom in the United States?

Organization

Is your paper divided into paragraphs?

Do the paragraphs have clear topics?

Do the paragraphs have topic sentences?

Grammar

Did you choose the correct verb tense for each verb?

Did you use the correct endings for each verb?

Did you form negative sentences correctly?

Did you use comparative adjectives correctly?

After you have finished rewriting your composition, give it to your teacher.

Reading 2: Academic Reading

This reading is similar to a section of a textbook in economics. It is about the economic life of immigrants.

A Better Life for Immigrants?

1   Most of the people in the world who leave their country and immigrate to a new country come to the United States. Is their life better? Did those people make a good decision? We can answer this question in many ways. One way is to think about economic topics such as income, which is how much money people earn. We can also answer this question by looking at housing, the homes where people live.

Income

2   One part of the field of economics is the study of *income*, that is, how much money people make from their work. Economists (the people who study about economics) study the income of different groups of people. There are many studies of the income of immigrant groups in the United States.

3   Many immigrants come to the United States for economic reasons. They come because they hope to earn more money. Incomes in the United States are higher than they are in many other countries. Immigrants want to come to the United States for higher income.

4   However, immigrants are sometimes disappointed about their income in the United States. Foreign-born people often do not earn the same wages as people who were born in this country. Here is an example: the median, or "middle" salary of all full-time workers in the United States in 2002 was about $35,000. The median salary for foreign-born workers was about $27,000. For non-citizens, it was even lower, about $23,000.

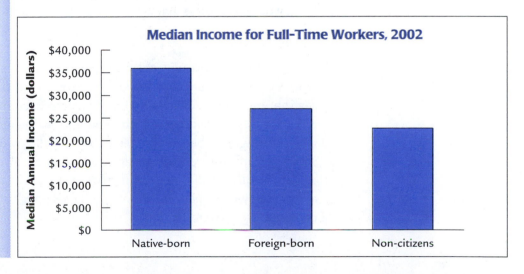

5   The income of foreign-born people is lower than the income of other people in the United States, but it is higher than the income in many other countries. Which is more important? Immigrants have to answer this question for themselves.

6   There is some good news about the lower wages that foreign-born workers earn. As immigrants spend more time in the United States, their wages go up more quickly. Also, the children of foreign-born workers earn more than their parents. They start to catch up with the wages of people whose parents were born here.

7   Here is an example of how immigrant families catch up with native-born families over time. In the early twentieth century, the income of immigrants was much lower than the income of other groups. For every dollar that a native-born person earned, immigrants earned only seventy cents. Over time, the difference, or the "gap," between the income of immigrants and the income of native-born people became smaller.

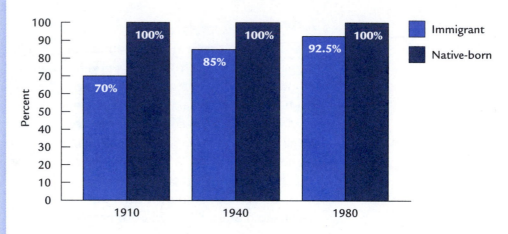

Income of Native-born and Immigrant Workers, 1910–1980

8   Immigrants earn less because of the jobs that they have. Foreign-born workers often work in jobs that have the lowest pay. There are more immigrants in jobs such as cleaning houses and working on farms. There are fewer foreign-born workers who are managers or have other high-paying jobs.

Homeownership

9   Economists also study where people live. They look at the number of people who rent their homes, and how many people own their own homes. Economists say that more homeownership means a better economy.

10   For immigrants, there is both good and bad news. The good news is that when immigrants become citizens, they usually own their homes. About sixty-seven percent of foreign-born citizens own their own home.

11   On the other hand, most non-citizens do not own their own home. Only about thirty-three percent of non-citizens own a home. This is very low compared to citizens.

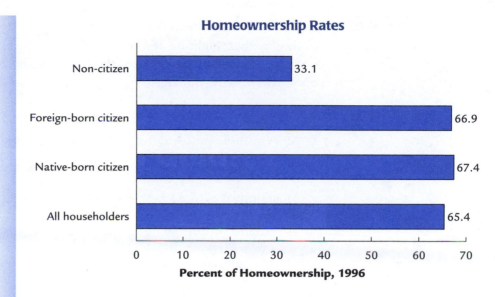

Homeownership Rates

	Percent
Non-citizen	33.1
Foreign-born citizen	66.9
Native-born citizen	67.4
All householders	65.4

Percent of Homeownership, 1996

12   The economic life of immigrants has both positive and negative parts. In many cases, economic life for new immigrants is very hard. On the other hand, many immigrants do well when they become U.S. citizens. Economists help us understand more clearly both the positive and negative sides of immigration to the United States.

Vocabulary

ACTIVITY 11   You probably already know the words below. To check your understanding of these words, choose one of the words to fit in each sentence. After you are done, review your answers with your class.

earn (verb)   **gap** (noun)
disappointed (adjective)   **manager** (noun)
century (noun)

1. We thought we were going to find good jobs with high salaries. When we did not find them, we were _____.

2. The boss understands how to help people work better. She knows how to lead the employees. She is a good _____.

3. That building stood for a hundred years. It was there for a _____.

4. My salary is more than $2,000 a month. I _____ about $25,000 a year.

5. There is a big difference between the salaries of immigrants and non-immigrants. Economists study this _____ in income.

Academic Words Read the sample sentences. They contain academic vocabulary that might be new to you. Then, in the sentences that follow, choose the academic word in **boldface** that fits best in each sentence. Review your answers with your class.

1. People who leave one country and move to a new country are **immigrants**.

2. An **economic** problem is a problem that is connected with money.

3. **Income** is the amount of money that a person earns.

a. The family is earning more money this year than last year. This is an

_____ improvement.

b. They became citizens last year, but they were not born here. They are

_____.

c. I have to increase the money I earn. I need a higher _____.

Discussion

Discuss these questions with your class.

1. Are you surprised about the difference in the salaries that native-born and foreign-born workers make? What do you think are the reasons for this difference?

2. Are you surprised about the number of citizens and non-citizens who own their homes? What do you think are the reasons for this difference?

3. Did it surprise you to read that the children of immigrants usually earn more than their parents, and that they have income closer to the income of native-born U.S. citizens? How can you explain this change?

Composition Analysis

Positive and Negative Information About a Topic Reading 2 presents economic information that relates to immigrants. The two economic topics are *income* and *homeownership*. There are two headings in the reading that show where information about these topics is contained.

Each of these two sections has both positive and negative information for immigrants. There are separate paragraphs for both the "good news" and the "bad news" about economic topics. In order to understand the reading well, you should be able to find both positive and negative information about each topic.

Analyze the positive and negative economic information in Reading 2, and record the information in the chart below. (The first two are done for you.) Note the paragraph number where the information appears. Review your analysis with your class.

Income		
Positive	Negative	Paragraph
Income in the United States is higher than in other countries.		3, 5
	Foreign-born workers earn less; non-citizens earn even less.	4

Homeownership		
Positive	Negative	Paragraph

Writing 2

ACTIVITY 15

In the writing assignment for this chapter, you will be writing about what life is like for immigrants in the United States. To prepare for the assignment, review Readings 1 and 2, and write sentences about the questions below.

Jobs and income: Are good jobs available for immigrants?

_____

_____

_____

Places to live: Is it possible for immigrants to own a home?

_____

_____

_____

Help from others: Do you feel that people in the United States want to help immigrants?

_____

_____

_____

Crime and fear: Is crime in the United States a problem that seriously affects immigrants' lives?

_____

_____

_____

ACTIVITY 16

Writing Assignment Write a composition about what life is like for immigrants in the United States. Imagine that you are writing to people who have never been here. What do you want to tell them about this country? What are the good things and what are the bad things? What advice can you give to people who are thinking about coming here? You can include information from Reading 2 and from your own experience. Use your answers from Activity 15 to help you.

Grammar

Contrast Expressions

In Reading 2, there are two expressions that show contrast between the ideas in two sentences or paragraphs: *however* and *on the other hand*. At the beginning of paragraph 4, *however* shows that the ideas in this paragraph are different from the ideas in paragraph 3.

At the beginning of paragraph 11, we see the expression *on the other hand*. This also shows a contrast with the ideas in paragraph 10.

In Chapter 5, you studied other contrast expressions, such as *but* and *although*. Remember that those expressions are used to put together two parts of a sentence:

Income is higher in the United States, **but** jobs are difficult to find.

However and *on the other hand* use different punctuation from *but* and *although*. *However* and *on the other hand* should both have a comma **after** them.

My sister writes well in English. **However**, she does not know how to write in our parents' home language.

My dog is extremely friendly. **On the other hand**, my cat is afraid of new people.

As you may remember, *but* usually has a comma **before** it.

I love chocolate, **but** it makes me sick.

Although in the middle of a sentence usually has no comma or other punctuation. In longer sentences, sometimes writers use a comma before *although*.

I love chocolate **although** it makes me sick.

ACTIVITY 17

Use these contrast expressions to show the differences between each pair of ideas in four different ways. The first one is done for you as an example.

| **however,** | **on the other hand,** | **, but** | **although** |

Income of new immigrants is low.
Income is higher than it was in their home country.

1. *The income of new immigrants is low. However, it is higher than it was in their home country.*

2. *The income of new immigrants is low. On the other hand, it is higher than it was in their home country.*

3. _The income of new immigrants is low, but it is higher than it was_

   in their home country.

4. _The income of new immigrants is low although it is higher than_

   it was in their home country.

Many immigrants who are citizens own their own homes.
Not many non-citizens are homeowners.

1. _____

   _____

2. _____

   _____

3. _____

   _____

4. _____

   _____

Foreign-born immigrants often make low wages.
Their children will often make higher wages than they did.

1. _____

   _____

2. _____

   _____

3. _____

   _____

4. _____

   _____

The sentences below have some mistakes in contrast expressions, especially in their punctuation. Find the mistakes and make corrections. Discuss your answers with your class.

1. I live in a safe neighborhood, on the other hand some of my friends do not.

2. She has lived here for a long time. Although she cannot afford a house.

3. He earns more than he earned last year. But he still would like to earn more.

4. However they have a big family, it seems that everyone is too busy to help.

Rewriting 2

ACTIVITY 19 Use the checklist below to review the important parts of your composition. If the answer to any of the questions is "no," make changes when you rewrite your paper. After you are finished making changes, give your composition to your teacher.

CHECKLIST

Content
Does your composition about life in the United States include your opinion about jobs and income, good places to live, help from people around you, and crime?

Organization
Is your paper divided into paragraphs?

Do the paragraphs have clear topics?

Do the paragraphs have topic sentences?

Grammar
Did you choose the correct verb tense for each verb?

Did you use the correct endings for each verb?

Did you form negative sentences correctly?

Did you use comparison expressions correctly?

Did you use expressions to show contrast between ideas correctly?

Internet Activities

For additional activities related to this chapter, go to elt.thomson.com/catalyst.

8 A Better World Through Sports?

Exploring the Topic

ACTIVITY 1

Discussion Discuss these questions with a partner. Your teacher may ask you to report what you discussed.

1. Do you watch sports, either in person or on TV? Do you have positive or negative feelings about sports?

2. Do you think people in the United States have a good opinion or a bad opinion about you when they first meet you because of your nationality? What are some positive or negative feelings that people here have about your ethnic group?

PART 1

Reading 1: Personal Experience Reading

This story is told by Dolores. She is a middle-aged woman who has lived in the United States for about ten years. She lives with her husband Carlos and their son Luis in Boston. They live in a neighborhood where most of the people come from the United States.

Read Dolores's story. When you come to the end, notice that the story is not finished. You will have questions about what will happen next.

A Door into a New Life

1   I remember when we first came to Boston from Santo Domingo. My husband Carlos and I were really excited about our new lives here, but we were a little nervous, too. It seems so long ago now. We bought the house, and that seemed great, but we felt separated from other people. We did not talk to our neighbors very much, except to say hello.

2   Our son Luis was going to high school. I think he felt kind of lost. He was always a good student, but of course he was having a hard time with English at first. He studied English in our country, but it was so different for him here. He always felt like he was behind the other students. Sometimes we wondered if all of this change was really fair to him.

3   Luis came home one day and said he had joined the soccer team at school. He wanted us to sign a form. Carlos and I were not sure it was a good idea. Luis

was having a hard time with his grades, and we thought he needed the time to study. However, he really wanted to do it, so we said it was OK if his grades did not go down.

4   Luis didn't talk about the team much at first. Then one day he asked us to watch him play. The game was on a Saturday morning. We were free and we were also kind of curious about what he was doing, so we decided to go.

5   I don't remember a lot about the game that day, but one thing really stayed with me. That was the day we met Barb and Joe. I was not really trying to meet people or make friends. I remember during the game that one of the players on our team put the ball in the net. All the parents on our side started to cheer, but then the referee said it was not a goal. I said to myself, in Spanish, "Fuera de juego." I was really talking to myself. The other parents were kind of going crazy. They wanted to know why the goal was no good. I remember my English was really terrible. I did not know him, but Joe turned to me and asked me what I said. I tried to explain: "It's no good! He was too early. He was alone when he got the ball." I didn't know the English word for the rule about "offside."

6   After everyone calmed down, Joe and Barb came to talk to me, and to Carlos. Joe said, "From now on, I'm going to stand next to you during the games. I want to know what's going on!" We did come to another game, and we talked to Barb and Joe again. I am not an expert on soccer at all, but I know a little bit. They didn't know anything! They stayed close to Carlos and me so they could ask questions. We started to come to all the games, and we became "soccer friends" with the other parents, especially Barb and Joe. It was a little bit hard for us, since we were the only foreigners, and the only Spanish speakers. We were friendly during the games and we discussed the kids a little bit, but when the games were over, we said, "See you next week," and that was it.

7   I admit that I had an idea about Americans at that time, an idea that was not very good. I thought they were all very unfriendly. It seemed to me that the other parents thought they were a little bit better than us. They didn't do anything bad, but they seemed so cold.

8   This coldness bothered me a lot, because I am a very open and friendly person. I like to talk. I don't like to say only "hello" and "goodbye" to people. I enjoy getting to know them more. Of course, Carlos is completely different. He is very quiet, and he does not care if people want to talk to him. This problem of feeling separated from people was really my problem, not his.

9   At the end of the season, we felt kind of shy when we said goodbye to the other families. I thought we would not see each other anymore, at least until next fall. I wrote our phone number on a piece of paper and I gave it to Barb.

Vocabulary

ACTIVITY 2 You probably already know the words below. To check your understanding of these words, choose one of the words to fit in the sentences that follow. After you are done, review your answers with your class.

excited (adjective)   **cheered** (verb)
curious (adjective)   **calmed down** (verb)

1. The people _____ when they understood the problem.

2. They _____ so loudly that no one could hear what was happening.

3. I did not know anything about it, but I was _____ to find out more.

4. They got _____ when they heard that we had won.

ACTIVITY 3 **Academic Words** Read the sample sentences. They contain academic vocabulary in **boldface** that might be new to you. Then, in the sentences that follow, choose the academic word that fits best in the sentence. Review your answers with your class.

1. A **grade** is the level or the quality of something. Teachers use **grades** to describe the quality of their students' work.

2. When people decide to do something difficult that they did not do before, they set a **goal**. A **goal** is also used in several sports. It is the place that the players are trying to put the ball during a game, or success in getting the ball into that place.

3. An **expert** is someone who knows a lot about a subject or topic.

a. She is an _____ on American history. She has written several books on the subject.

b. She studied hard all semester. As a result, her _____ improved.

c. He wants to improve his speaking ability. That is his _____ for the semester.

Discussion

Discuss these questions with your class.

1. Do you think it was a good idea for Luis to join the soccer team? Why or why not?

2. Dolores says that the other families at the soccer games were "soccer friends." What do you think she means by this?

3. What do you think will happen to Dolores's family in the future?

Composition Analysis

Paragraphs and Topics: Chronological Order As you saw in other chapters, Reading 1 in this chapter is a narration about personal experiences. The topic of each paragraph is a different set of events, and the paragraphs are organized in order according to the time when they happened. This kind of order, following time, is called **chronological order**.

ACTIVITY 5 Dolores's story has nine paragraphs. Each paragraph has a topic, and the paragraphs are organized mostly in chronological order. First, read the list of topics below. Write the number of the paragraph in Reading 1 that has a topic closest to the given topic.

_____ Dolores's and Carlos's personalities

_____ How Dolores started talking to the other parents the first time

_____ Luis's problems at school

_____ How Dolores felt about Americans

_____ What happened at the end of the season

_____ How Luis joined the soccer team at school

_____ How Dolores felt when she first came to the United States

_____ How Luis invited his parents to see a soccer game

_____ How Dolores started to become friendly with Barb and Joe and the other parents

ACTIVITY 6 In your writing assignment for this section, you will be writing your ideas about the future of Dolores and her family. Discuss these questions with a classmate, then write answers in the form of sentences.

1. Will the friendship between Dolores's family and Barb and Joe's family continue?

   _____

   _____

2. Will Dolores change her feelings about Americans?

   _____

   _____

3. What will happen with Luis and his problems at school?

   _____

   _____

ACTIVITY 7 **Writing Assignment** Write a paper in which you tell about the future of Dolores, Carlos, and Luis. First, give a short summary of what you know about Dolores and the other members of her family. Also give a short summary of how Dolores met Barb and Joe. Then write about the future. Will Dolores's friendship with Barb and Joe continue after soccer season, or will it end? Will Dolores change her feelings about Americans and their "coldness"? What will happen with Luis and his problems in school? Explain the reasons for your ideas or opinions.

Grammar

Verb Tenses: Future Tense

Your answers to the questions in Activity 6 and your composition about Dolores and her family are about the future. In these activities, your writing might include sentences like this:

> Dolores and her family **will continue** their friendship with Barb and Joe's family.
> Dolores **will change** her thinking about American people.

The verbs in these sentences are in the **future tense**. Notice the form of these verbs: there is an auxiliary verb *will*, and then the base form of the main verb, such as *continue* or *change*. Notice that the form of *will* does not change, even if the subject of the sentence changes from *they* to *she*. This rule is the same as the rule for modal verbs that you saw in the Grammar section in Chapter 2, Part 1, and Chapter 3, Part 2.

You can use *not* to make negative sentences in the future tense. The word *not* follows *will* in sentences about the future. For example:

> Luis **will not improve** his work in school.

ACTIVITY 8

Write sentences that tell about your future. For each item, write a sentence that describes your future. In each sentence, use *will* and the base form of the verb. The first one is done as an example.

tomorrow *Tomorrow I will go to work in the morning.* _____

next summer _____

next year _____

in ten years _____

ACTIVITY 9

The paragraphs below have some mistakes in future tense verb forms. Find the mistakes and make corrections. (You should find four mistakes.) Discuss your answers with your class.

I think Dolores's friendship with Barb and Joe will continuing. They like each other, and they both have nice families. The friendship no will end. I think Dolores also will change her feelings about Americans. If she spends more time in this country, she wills not feel that Americans are so cold. I also think that Luis will improves in school. He is smart, and he has a good family. He will do well.

Rewriting 1

ACTIVITY 10 Review the composition you wrote in Activity 7. Find examples of future tense verbs, or places where you should use future tense. Make corrections in the form of these verbs where you need to.

You can use the checklist below to help you review the other important things you need to include in your composition. If your answer to any of the questions is "no," make changes to your paper. When you are finished, give your paper to your teacher.

CHECKLIST

Content

Is there a short summary about Dolores and the other members of her family?

Is there a short summary of how Dolores met Barb and Joe?

Did you write about the future, including what will happen with the friendship with Barb and Joe, Dolores's feelings about Americans, and Luis and his problems in school?

Organization

Is your paper divided into paragraphs?

Do the paragraphs have clear topics?

Do the paragraphs have topic sentences?

Grammar

Did you choose the correct verb tense for each verb?

Did you form each verb tense correctly, including future tense?

PART 2

Reading 2: Academic Reading

This reading is about the good effects that sports can have on society.

More Than a Game

1   Most people think of sports as something to do for fun, or as a way to get exercise. However, in some cases people use sports as a way to improve society. In many places in the world, people hope that sports can bring together people from different social groups.

2   In some countries, people are using sports as one way to solve social problems. In South Africa, for example, the history of racism still causes deep problems between black and white people. Now, special training for sports teachers and coaches helps them understand racial problems. The idea of the project is for young people from different groups to work together as a team. This can be a step toward working together in other parts of life. In Bulgaria, a soccer team was recently made up of young people from two ethnic groups, Bulgarians and Romany people. In Bulgaria, there is a history of discriminating against the Romany[1] people. The new soccer team toured Bulgaria and tried to show people in that country that the two groups could live and work together. In Europe, the "Homeless World Cup" is an international program that brings homeless people into soccer teams. The program uses the games as a way to bring attention to the needs of homeless people.

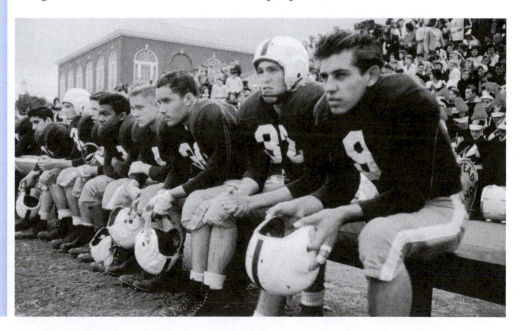

[1] *Romany* people are also sometimes called "Gypsies." Some people feel that this name is insulting.

3   Sports teach values that can be useful in bringing people together. Most sports include ideas about fairness. Some people believe that ideas about "fair play" in a game can translate into ideas about fairness for minority groups. If young people can learn ideas about fair play in a game, they can use the same ideas in other situations, such as in school or at work.

4   Sports can also bring people together because they teach important social skills. These skills include working as a group, and tolerating those who are different. There is an American football team in Illinois that has several Muslim students. Although the majority of students on the team are not Muslims, the coaches have changed the routine of the team to make things easier for the Muslim players. For example, Muslims fast[2] in the daytime during Ramadan, a holy month in the Muslim religion. This month always comes in the most important part of the football season. The coaches make special efforts to allow the Muslim students to eat at sundown after their fast. The coaches also allow Muslim players to take a break from practice to pray. They believe that the other players learn to understand and respect the Muslim students when they see how difficult it is to follow their traditions.

5   Psychologists believe that when a group has the same wish to succeed, they are more likely to work together and succeed. However, being on a team, even a successful team, does not mean that differences or problems between groups will disappear off the field. This is because a close social connection is not necessary for teams to succeed. Research shows that members of successful teams sometimes do not like each other or get along. However, they can put their bad feelings aside during a game. A famous example is the American basketball team, the Chicago Bulls. They were the most successful team in the country in the 1990s, yet they did not speak to each other away from practices and games. People can feel positive about each other as the result of sports teams, but just because they play sports with members of another group, they will not automatically learn tolerance. Sports can only bring people together if athletes and coaches work at it as part of a program.

6   One of the most famous stories that connects sports and society is the life story of Jackie Robinson. He was the first black man to play for a Major League baseball team in the United States. He was a star player for the Brooklyn Dodgers from 1956 until 1966. When he started to play as a professional, many baseball fans believed that a black man should not be allowed to play on a team of mostly white players. When he joined the Dodgers and became one of the greatest players ever, some white people changed their minds. They changed their minds about black people in sports, and then changed their other negative ideas about black people in general.

7   However, the Jackie Robinson story was not an accident. For years before Robinson joined the team, the manager of the Dodgers team worked with a group of black leaders, social scientists, and politicians. They planned the best way to bring a black person into baseball. This group discussed exactly what kind of personality the first black player should have, and they talked about ways to encourage white people to accept the change.

---

[2] *Fast* means to stop eating or drinking for a special purpose, often as part of a religion.

8   Some people believe that the sport of soccer has a special role in bringing people together. It is the most popular game in the world, and almost every country in the world has soccer teams. In the United States, soccer can help immigrants to feel a part of life in their new country. The game came to the United States in the 1800s, when most of the players were immigrants from England and Ireland. In the past, many U.S. soccer teams were for people from one ethnic group, but today teams often have people from different groups. In the past, soccer was not popular in the United States, partly because people connected the game with immigrants. Its popularity increased in the 1970s when the famous Brazilian star Pele came to New York and played for a professional team. Youth soccer is now bigger in the United States than youth baseball, and it includes millions of kids every year. Now that soccer is more popular in the United States, people often look to immigrants as the best players and teachers.

9   As more people come to the United States from other parts of the world, tolerance becomes important to more people. It is possible that sharing social activities such as sports, music, and food will help people see members of other groups in a more positive way, so that we can share our complicated, changing country.

Vocabulary

ACTIVITY 11   You probably already know the words below. To check your understanding of these words, choose one of the words to fit in each sentence. After you are done, review your answers with your class.

solve (verb)   skills (noun)
toured (verb)   pray (verb)
international (adjective) connection (noun)
attention (noun)   aside (adverb)

1. They practiced hard and improved their _____.

2. She paid _____ to all of her children.

3. They _____ during the religious holiday.

4. The purpose of the program was to _____ social problems.

5. I had to put _____ my unhappiness and remember the good things.

6. The game was part of an _____ tour through Europe.

7. They visited ten countries when they _____ Africa.

8. They saw a _____ between fair play in sports and in society.

Academic Words Read the sample sentences. They contain academic vocabulary in **boldface** that might be new to you. Then, in the sentences that follow, choose the academic word that fits best in each sentence. Review your answers with your class.

1. If something happens **automatically**, no one planned it or thought about it before that time.

2. If a person **discriminates** against another group of people, he or she does something negative to them only because of the group they belong to.

3. An **ethnic** group is a group of people with the same nationality or culture.

4. A **majority** is a group that makes up more than half of a larger group.

5. A **minority** is a group that makes up less than half of a larger group.

6. A **professional** activity is paid work. A **professional** musician or athlete receives money for work in music or sports.

7. **Psychologists** study the science of human behavior.

8. **Research** is activity that tries to find the answer to an important question.

9. A **role** is a job or a part that a person has in a group.

10. **Traditions** are ideas or actions of members of a social group, such as an ethnic group.

a. When I heard the noise, I _____ jumped.

b. English speakers are a _____ in the United States.

c. People bring some of their culture and _____ when they immigrate to a new country.

d. The new test _____ against people who have no education.

e. _____ clubs always have members of the same nationality.

f. She is a _____ photographer. Her photos have appeared in many magazines.

g. Italian speakers are a _____ in the United States.

h. _____ believe that people can succeed together when they have the same goal.

i. The _____ showed that sports can help people to learn tolerance.

j. The _____ of a teacher is to help students find their best ways to learn.

Discussion

ACTIVITY 13 Discuss these questions with a classmate. Your teacher may ask you to report your answers to the class.

1. Do you play a sport, or enjoy watching a sport on television or in person?

2. Do you know of any situations where playing together in sports has helped people from different groups understand each other or get along with each other better?

3. According to the reading, people who work together do not need to like each other in order to succeed. In your experience, is this true?

Composition Analysis

Main Ideas and Examples Each paragraph in Reading 2 has its own topic and main idea. In some paragraphs, there are several examples that explain the main idea. Paragraph 2, for example, begins like this:

2   In some countries, people are using sports as one way to solve social problems.

In the rest of the paragraph, we see examples of this idea from South Africa, Bulgaria, and Europe:

... In **South Africa**, for example, the history of racism still causes deep problems between black and white people. Now, special training for sports teachers and coaches helps them understand racial problems. The idea of the project is for young people from different groups to work together as a team. This can be a step toward working together in other parts of life. In **Bulgaria**, a soccer team was recently made up of young people from two ethnic groups, Bulgarians and Romany people. In Bulgaria, there is a history of discriminating against the Romany people. The new soccer team toured Bulgaria, and tried to show people in that country that the two groups could live and work together. In **Europe**, the "Homeless World Cup" is an international program that brings homeless people into soccer teams. The program uses the games as a way to bring attention to the needs of homeless people.

When you read academic writing, you can use the examples to understand the main idea of a paragraph.

Reading 2 has nine paragraphs. In some paragraphs, there are one or more examples that explain more about the main idea. Find the topic sentence in each paragraph of Reading 2 listed below. Write the main idea presented in the topic sentence of the paragraph and one example that explains that main idea.

Paragraph 3

Main idea: _____

Example: _____

_____

Paragraph 4

Main idea: _____

Example: _____

_____

Paragraph 5

Main idea: _____

Example: _____

_____

Paragraph 8

Main idea: _____

Example: _____

_____

Discuss your answers with your class.

ACTIVITY 15   In the writing assignment for this section, you will write about belonging to a group. Write answers below to these questions about the topic.

What group do you belong to with a purpose or activity that is shared by the group: An academic class? A club? A school? A workplace? A country?

_____

_____

What situations or behavior by this group made it hard to become part of the group?

_____

_____

_____

What experiences were helpful in becoming part of the group?

_____

_____

_____

ACTIVITY 16   **Writing Assignment** Write a composition that describes your experiences in becoming part of a group. The group could be a new class, a new school, a new workplace, a new country, a new sports team, a new religion, or some other type of group. What activities or behavior, by you or by other people, made it easier for you to join the group? What made things harder? Use your answers to Activity 15 above to help you as you write.

Grammar

Review of Verb Tenses

Reading 1 in this chapter, Dolores's story, is mainly a narration about the things that happened when her son joined his school's soccer team. Most of the verbs in this part of her story are in the simple past tense, for example:

> We **bought** the house.
> He **studied** English in our country.
> He **needed** the time to study.
> We **said** it was OK.
> Joe and Barb **came** to talk to me.
> We **started** to come to all the games.
> We **became** "soccer friends" with the other parents.
> It **was** a little bit hard for us.
> We **discussed** the kids a little bit.
> I **had** an idea about Americans.
> I **thought** they were all very unfriendly.
> We **felt** kind of shy.
> I **gave** it to Barb.

Some of the sentences are negative. Notice that they have *did not* or *didn't* before the verb:

> We **did not talk** to our neighbors.
> His grades **did not go** down.

Some of the sentences in the story describe Dolores and Carlos and their personalities. The verbs in these sentences are in the simple present tense:

> **I am** a very open and friendly person.
> **I don't like** to say only "hello" and "goodbye" to people.
> He **does not care** if people want to talk to him.

In Reading 2, many of the sentences describe things that are generally true. These sentences are in the simple present tense:

people **think**	sports **teach**
training **helps**	research **shows**
psychologists **believe**	members **do not like**
the history of racism **causes**	

There also is some narration in Reading 2, in paragraphs 6, 7, and 8. Many of the verbs in these paragraphs are in the simple past tense:

the team **toured**	he **became**
they **did not speak**	its popularity **increased**
people **connected**	Pele **came**
he **joined**	

ACTIVITY 17 Re-read Readings 1 and 2 and look at all the verbs. Underline each simple present tense verb once. Underline each simple past tense verb twice. Circle each future tense verb. Review your answers with your class.

ACTIVITY 18 The paragraphs below have some mistakes in the verb tenses. Find the mistakes and make corrections. (You should find ten mistakes.) Discuss your answers with your class.

When I first was started this class a few months ago, I'm very nervous. I thought that I not know as much about English or writing as the other students. I was away from school for many years.

The other students were nice, but they were not really friendly. Most of them were not from my country, and we did not had very much to talk about. I was older than most of the students, so I thought they do not want to talk to me.

Over time, the feeling in the class was change. The teacher was very friendly, and this helped us to relax. We working together in class every day, and we started to become closer.

I am not friendly with all of the students in the class. However, we still works together very well. We can to study together even if we are not friends. This is because we all want the same thing: we want to improve our English.

When the class is over, I think I will feel sad about it. I will be miss the other students and the good feeling we had together as a class.

Rewriting 2

ACTIVITY 19 Use the checklist below to answer questions about your paper from Activity 16. If the answer to any of the questions is "no," make changes in your paper. When you are finished, give your paper to your teacher.

> **CHECKLIST**
>
> **Content**
>
> Did you describe the experience of belonging to a group?
>
> Did you describe the situations and actions that made it harder to feel part of the group?
>
> Did you describe the things that made it easier to join the group?
>
> **Organization**
>
> Is your paper divided into paragraphs?
>
> Do the paragraphs have clear topics?
>
> Do the paragraphs have topic sentences?
>
> **Grammar**
>
> Did you choose the correct verb tense for each verb?
>
> Did you form each verb tense correctly? (Pay special attention to simple present tense, simple past tense, and future tense.)

Internet Activities

For additional activities related to this chapter, go to elt.thomson.com/catalyst.

Vocabulary

These are the words presented in Vocabulary and Academic Words sections. The part of speech is shown as the word is used in the text. Numbers following each word show the chapters in which the words appear.

 A

abandoned (adjective) 3
advise (verb) 2
affect (verb) 1
afford (verb) 5
affordable (adjective) 5
afraid (adjective) 2
angry (adjective) 2, 6
annoyed (adjective) 5
apart (adverb) 1
appreciate (verb) 3
approve (verb) 2
area (noun) 3, 5
argument (noun) 7
arrest (verb) 6
aside (adverb) 8
ask permission (verb) 7
attention (noun) 8
attitude (noun) 2
attraction (noun) 2
attractive (adjective) 5
automatically (adverb) 8
aware (adjective) 3

B

background (noun) 3
basket (noun) 3
beans (noun) 3
behavior (noun) 1, 6
border (noun) 3
borrow (verb) 4
bottom (noun) 3
bowl (noun) 3

brick (noun) 5
bunch (noun) 3

 C

calm down (verb) 8
century (noun) 7
cheat (verb) 6
cheer (verb) 8
civil (adjective) 6
climb (verb) 5
combine (verb) 2
commitment (noun) 2
commit (verb) 6
community (noun) 3, 4, 6
complain (verb) 6
concern (noun) 3
confident (adjective) 2
connection (noun) 8
contrasting (adjective) 2
contribute (verb) 3
corner (noun) 7
create (verb) 2, 3
crime (noun) 6
culture (noun) 2, 4
curious (adjective) 8
custom (noun) 5, 6

D

depression (noun) 4
depressed (adjective) 4
design (noun) 5
disappointed (adjective) 7
disapproval (noun) 2
discriminate (verb) 8

E

earn (verb) 7
economic (adjective) 7
edge (noun) 4
embarrassed (adjective) 1
empty (adjective) 4
energy (noun) 3
enjoys himself (verb) 1
environment (noun) 1, 5
especially (adverb) 3
ethnic (adjective) 4, 8
excited (adjective) 3, 8
expert (noun) 2, 8
express (verb) 3

F

feature (noun) 5
fence (noun) 3
finally (adverb) 5
flexible (adjective) 2
float (verb) 3
frighten (verb) 6

G

gap (noun) 7
goal (noun) 2, 8
government (noun) 3, 4, 6
grade (noun) 8
guest (noun) 5
guilty (adjective) 2

H

habit (noun) 2
honest (adjective) 6
hunting (noun) 6

I

identical (adjective) 1
image (noun) 7
imitates (verb) 3
immigrant (noun) 3, 4, 7
immigrate (verb) 4
immigration (noun) 4
improve (verb) 3
income (noun) 4, 7

increase (noun and verb) 3
international (adjective) 8

K

knife (noun) 6

L

leather (noun) 4
loan (verb and noun) 4
local (adjective) 3
lock (verb) 7

M

majority (noun) 8
manager (noun) 7
meal (noun) 7
minority (noun) 8
mistake (noun) 7
motive (noun) 2
movement (noun) 3
murder (noun) 6

O

occupation (noun) 3

P

pack (noun) 6
panels (noun) 3
participate (verb) 3
partner (noun) 2
permanent (adjective) 5
permission (noun) 7
pipe (noun) 4
positive (adjective) 3
practical (adjective) 2
pray (verb) 8
prayer (noun) 3
prejudice (noun) 2
pride (noun) 3
prison (noun) 6
process (noun) 3
professional (adjective) 3, 8
program (noun) 3
psychologist (noun) 1, 8
punish (verb) 6

R

railroad (noun) 5
recommended (verb) 5
remind (verb) 5
repair (noun and verb) 4, 5
research (noun) 8
resident (noun) 3
risk (noun and verb) 1, 7
role (noun) 8
roof (noun) 4, 5

S

salary (noun) 4
section (noun) 3
secure (adjective) 5
security (noun) 2
serious (adjective) 1
shocked (adjective) 5
shout (verb) 6
shy (adjective) 1
similar (adjective) 2, 3
situation (noun) 3
skill (noun) 8
slave (noun) 5
solution (noun) 5, 6
solve (verb) 8
style (noun) 3, 5
steep (adjective) 5
swings (noun) 5

T

temporary (adjective) 5
threaten (verb) 6
tour (verb) 8
traditional (adjective) 2
tradition (noun) 8

V

violence (noun) 6

W

weapon (noun) 6
witness (noun) 6
worried (adjective) 2
worry (verb) 1
worse (adjective) 2, 6

Y

yard (noun) 5

Irregular Verbs and Past Tense Forms

Base Form	Past Tense Form
be	was, were
become	became
begin	began
build	built
buy	bought
catch	caught
choose	chose
come	came
do	did
fall	fell
feel	felt
fight	fought
find	found
give	gave
go	went
have	had
know	knew
leave	left
lose	lost
meet	met
say	said
see	saw
speak	spoke
spend	spent
take	took
teach	taught
think	thought
understand	understood
write	wrote